Occupy WALL STREET

Revolution Handbook

The Unauthorized Collector's Edition

By Occupy Wall Street Activists

"Occupy Wall Street Revolution Handbook,
The Unauthorized Collector's Edition"

Another book from Occupy Wall Street Activists

Copyright © 2011, By Occupy Wall Street Activists

Fix Bay Inc Publishing
A Division of Holy Wow Publishing

Activists, Occupy Wall Street

1. Politics 2. International policies

ISBN: 978-0-9838149-3-1

DEDICATION

To all oppressed and poor people, including those from the
weakened middle class

TABLE OF CONTENTS

CHAPTER 1
This book will change the world

This book is going to change world history for the better.

Such a statement might sound like a mighty tall order. But our growing domestic and international movement has amassed unstoppable power.

As a result, "we shall overcome" many hardships that face the vast majority of people worldwide. In order to accomplish this, we—the occupiers of Wall Street, plus cities, nations and continents worldwide—have vowed to embrace and adhere to the rules, tactics and strategies listed in this essential handbook.

All of our warriors worldwide are called "Occupy Soldiers." Each of us carries a copy of this handbook at all times, either as printed "dead-tree" paper publications, or in an e-reader form viewable via computers, cell phones or other electronic devices.

While our movement achieves continual successes on a local, national and international basis, all Occupy Soldiers use this handbook as their doctrine.

Just as important, each of our warriors has a responsibility to ensure that virtually every Occupy Movement advocate has access to this publication at all times.

Many of our most avowed warriors insist on memorizing this publication, before spreading the doctrine contained herein via word of mouth.

This seems logical, because the notorious "1 percent" of the population that controls a majority of the world's wealth will go to almost any length to prohibit or ban this book.

Anyone in possession of this handbook should remain fully aware at all times that some "1-percenters" will seek to have you executed for having this controversial publication. Many of the world's wealthiest people fear that those of us armed with the powerful information contained herein will overthrow or rob them of their possessions.

Throughout the course of human history, evil despots, dictators, regimes and demented political parties have decimated huge populations of protestors, rebels or perceived enemies of those holding governmental and monetary power.

Our growing armies of Occupy Soldiers worldwide know that a similar fate shall continue as a distinct possibility until the 1-Percenters are neutralized.

As a result, we expect that non-stop streams of our loyal and relentless members worldwide shall be slaughtered in the coming months and years until we overcome the oppressors. In the interim, many of us will be shot, hanged, electrocuted, drowned, starved, bombed, firebombed, poisoned or exterminated in a variety of other ways.

All along, however, the survivors among us shall press forward with our valiant effort until ultimate victory becomes ours.

All Occupy Soldiers are doves.

Yet avoid getting fooled into thinking that we are weak. You see, all true doves are much stronger emotionally and spiritually than their warring, battle-oriented adversaries.

Even before our overall movement received its "Occupy" name, our efforts spread lightning fast around the globe because our initial organizers showed courage.

Collectively and individually, we realize that times likely will become much more difficult for us all before our personal situations improve for the better.

Encased in this knowledge, we have learned through history that almost anything significant worth achieving takes great struggle and tribulation to accomplish.

CHAPTER 2
All Governments Have Failed

All governments and political systems have failed throughout the course of human history. The dismal failures have included communism, capitalism, democracies, dictatorships, socialism, fascism, anarchism and wide-spread empires.

11

Predictably, each of these forms of government have fallen flat, becoming ineffective, much of the time for two single primary reasons—greed and ignorance.

Consistently for thousands of years many of the wisest leaders have taught us that "money is the root of all evil."

All along, people in many cultures have been taught that "ignorance is bliss." Sadly, quite the opposite has remained true. Simply stated, ignorance means poverty, oppression and selfish, hateful, despicable deeds that open up the way for continued anguish.

The Politicians Have Failed Us

Worsening matters, all politicians have failed the citizens of the world—individually and collectively in virtually every nation and in all types of governments.

Today's Occupy Warriors realize this every step of the way. Until such time as our earth finds a solution, politicians have, are and will continue to fail us.

Although those of us in the Occupy movement are essentially doves, we recognize and acknowledge the fact that local, state, national and world leaders invariably fall flat.

Political polices implemented immediately before and after the onset of the 21st Century exacerbated social and economic problems on a massive worldwide scale.

Kiss-ass political leaders and candidates have promised everything from "hope" and "change" but delivered very little while offering few specifics.

The News Media Have Failed Us

Worsening matters, the news media have failed all types of governments and people in virtually every society.

Throughout history all forms of public communication and "news" dissemination have emerged as inadequate or deceptive to varying degrees.

During much of the 20th Century in propaganda disseminated in the form of supposed "news," those who give so-called event updates to the public have failed society everywhere from communist China and Russia, plus Nazi Germany.

Many of the worst failures within this realm kicked into full gear early in the 21st Century when greedy corporations took over the bulk of the mainstream U.S. news media. Giant money-hungry corporations slashed and obliterated news division budgets at newspapers, TV channels, television networks and radio stations.

These sharp cutbacks resulted in the severe curtailing or elimination of critical or important in-depth and highly revealing "news." Newsroom staffs that once boasted dozens of professional journalists now have less than a handful of rookie reporters that generate short, fluffy stories and insignificant, inconsequential "sound bites."

CHAPTER 3
Greedy Corporations Ignited the Problem

Greedy, money-hungry and impersonal corporations worldwide ignited the problems that caused widespread oppression of individuals and their families, especially during the 21st Century.

Compounding the problem, incompetent governments and inept politicians in many nations and throughout diverse cultures have essentially "gone to bed" with devilish Big Companies.

In almost every industrialized nation, governments have enacted legislation that favors huge corporations. These laws, in turn, have emerged in a virtual slap into the face of working people worldwide.

The worst results sprang forth in some of the world's former superpowers including the United States, Russia, China and Great Britain.

As slaves of the super-rich and powerful corporations, politicians worldwide enacted laws that: obliterated and decimated the middle-class; sent jobs overseas, destroyed entire national economies; gave tax breaks to only the wealthy, while leaving low-paid workers entrapped into a world of poverty; and enacted laws that favor only huge companies while paying little heed to the rights and needs of individuals and families.

Evil Lobbyists Exacerbate Problems

The proverbial hit-men and hit-women in this pernicious, harmful process are lobbyists. Most employed by corporations, these sneaky, sniveling professionals work behind-the-scenes to screw the little guy while helping giant companies and the Wealthy.

"You depend on the information that only we can provide," the most seasoned lobbyists tell politicians, who invariably do whatever they're told in order to retain their powerful positions in office.

The worst lobbyists work for: huge corporations that pollute the environment. While training politicians to "look the other way;" gigantic accounting firms and big tax preparation companies, all of them firms benefiting from confusing IRS codes manipulate: fascist conservatives who insist that big-government contracts should benefit private companies; and loony liberals who want to saddle taxpayers with the burden of paying the way for illegal immigrants or providing "free" houses for everyone who is poor.

Worsening matters, many lobbyists play an integral role in determining which politicians in democratic countries receive huge company-generated campaign donations from corporations or donations from political action committees commonly known as PACs.

Ultimately, these systems in democracies and semi-communist countries as well have resulted in governments that are corrupt. In fact, virtually all major governments in the world today are operated by crooks, including in China and Russia, plus particularly the United States.

Accountants and Lawyers Join the Corruption

Many of the most corrupt, behind-the-scenes professionals are lawyers and accountants who benefit greatly from convoluted laws. These vital and necessary segments of the economy, supported by their own high-paid lobbyists, work to enact legislation that ensures them high incomes and makes the public dependant on their slimy professions.

Capitalism, communism, socialism and dictatorships rise and fall step-for-step in many nations with the evil, self-centered mindset of bean counters and self-serving legal gurus.

Tearing deep into the fabric of many diverse cultures, wicked lawyers, crappy accountants and despotic lobbyists use cronyism and political one-upmanship to push their greedy tentacles deep into the hearts of many economies.

While the Rich pull the purse strings of these manipulators, this in turn plays in integral aspect is creating a ripple effect that plays a vital role in wiping out the middle-class.

Only the Rich and Poor Remain

Thanks to their mutual efforts, politicians and corporations worldwide have for the most part managed to wipe out the bulk of the middle-class.

With steadily increasing intensity, this has resulted in many cultures where average working-class people who once were able to earn a decent living have started to become extinct. Gone are the days when an average working couple could support a family fairly easily as both as they both held good jobs.

At a steadily increasing rate, the basic culture across the

United States and in many other nations worldwide has been left with only the very poor and the extremely Wealthy.

As a result, for the most part the former middle-class, now mostly relegated to being poor, find themselves "trampled upon" by the extremely powerful Rich elite.

CHAPTER 4
No one watched out for average people

As the governments in virtually every major industrialized country became increasingly corrupt during the early 21st Century, virtually no super-powerful lobbying organization worked to support the interests of the middle-class.

The expert professional lobbyists employed by huge corporations, lawyers, accounts and the Wealthy lobbied for: taxation laws that gave huge breaks to only the very wealthy; develop-at-any-cost legislation that ignored environmental concerns; and the overall enactment of policies that made the "rich richer and the poor poorer."

Lacking the necessary finances to politically back their own needs, and ignorant of what was happing to their governments, the middle class sunk further into the financial abyss. The dire situation became pernicious, essentially feeding upon itself.

Regular "working class" families in various cultures, in numerous countries and throughout many cultures found mere survival extremely difficult.

The situation worsened when huge corporations began to realize that the poor and downtrodden middle class had essentially become weak—essentially making them "easy targets" from which to make a quick, easy buck.

Banks and financial institutions became vultures

Eager to feed upon the weak and helpless throughout society, after the worldwide financial crisis clicked into full gear in 2009 and 2010, banks and financial institutions began to "feed" upon the weak, the under-represented poor and the shrinking middle class.

While backed by high-paid, powerful lobbyists in the U.S. Congress, U.S. Bank initially slapped checking account holders with a greedy, selfish $5-per-month fee when using a debit card during any 30-day period.

Eager to follow suit, numerous other banks in late 2011 became vultures, all of them announcing $3-per-month fees for similar debit-card use.

Amazingly, and sadly as well, the very financial institutions that taxpayers had bailed out to the tune of hundreds of billions of dollars following the financial crisis of 2008 were now starting to suck consumers dry.

The greed permeated worldwide, the average consumer left virtually helpless to change the course of corrupt governments everywhere. Thankfully, thanks to our Occupy Movement's loud voices in the autumn of 2011, the banks chickened out and backed off of their debit card fee plans, vowing to devise other ways of legally screwing the public out of their hard-earned cash.

Public servants were treated like criminals

The situation became even more disgusting on a national and worldwide scale when some politicians started treating public servants as if they were criminals.

Conservative politicians made public school teachers the subject of ridicule in several states, treating educators, police officers, firefighters and other law-abiding government employees as if lawbreakers for simply wanting decent wages.

Class warfare erupted when some elected leaders insisted on slashing the salaries of public workers, laying many of them off and obliterating their rights to bargain as unions.

As if to throw manure onto a proverbial cooling fan, meantime politicians in several states enacted cushy government pension programs benefiting only themselves.

CHAPTER 5
Financial institutions pecked like buzzards

Like exceedingly corrupt vultures, mindless and greedy financial institutions played the primary role in clicking the current worldwide financial crisis into full gear.

The world fell into a deep, prolonged and relentless recession in September 2008 when a scheme concocted by financial institutions worldwide finally collapsed.

The falls of Lehman Brothers and AIG, two mega-corporations focused on the financial industry, left millions of people worldwide homeless, unemployed and facing unstoppable home foreclosures.

The U.S. savings and loan industry crisis of the late 1980s, and the burst of the Internet stock bubble in 2001 paled by comparison.

In summary, the horrific and relentless current worldwide financial woes stem from lax, poorly regulated finance industry rules enacted by the U.S. Congress and other national governments—primarily during the 1990s.

Lobbyists and huge corporations created derivatives

Corrupt governments and political bodies including the U.S. Congress allowed investors to start trading newly created financial instruments called "derivatives" beginning in the final several years of the 20th Century.

In technical terms, these investments enabled corporations or wealthy speculators to essentially "bet" on what the values of underlying variables or securities would be at pre-designated dates. Some creative financiers used certain derivatives as a means of offering credit.

In the United States, a handful of politicians unsuccessfully attempted to enact legislation that would have regulated the trading of derivatives.

However, high-priced and well-connected lobbyists successfully worked to ensure that the Commodity Futures Modernization Act of 2000 de-regulate the trading of financial products such as the riskiest financial instruments.

Ultimately this legislation signed into law by then-President

Bill Clinton played an integral role in clearing the way for corrupt trading among financial institutions—eventually leading the way to the current, ongoing and persistent international financial crisis.

Common sense flew out the window

Boosted by their high-powered lobbying efforts, the financial industry managed to shoot down an attempt by the Commodity Futures Trading Commission to regulate derivatives. As a result, the world's largest financial institutions were able to engage in the now-infamous "credit default swap," essentially betting that loans would default.

Essentially left to their own devices, huge greedy and selfish corporations were then able to eagerly dole out mortgages to home buyers who should not have qualified for the loans—due to these individuals' insufficient incomes and poor credit.

An observer might easily say that the "little guy" was being played as a proverbial pawn in an international chess game. The only players were huge international financial institutions valued at hundreds of billions or trillions of dollars.

According to the International Swaps and Derivatives Association, the outstanding credit default swap or CDS swelled to a gargantuan $62.2 trillion in 2007. But the proverbial bubble essentially burst full force when corrupt or ignorant finance industry lenders gave far too many "bad loans" or mortgages to home buyers who never should have qualified.

As a result, as shown by the association's data, by mid-2010 the total CDS value had tumbled to $26.3 trillion—less than half the total from just two years earlier.

Ultimately, the people of the world had begun to suffer, all for the folly of the few reckless 1-Percenters who had once been rich enough to play the derivatives game.

21

CHAPTER 6
The Housing Crisis Sparked Anger

Sparking anger among a whopping 99 percent of the world's population, the selfish policies of bankers, financiers and investors sparked the international economic slump.

The prolonged downturn that clicked into full gear in 2008 served as a significant spark in igniting worldwide contempt, resulting in what many analysts call the Great Recession—a "lesser depression" or "long recession."

Among the former middle class and poor, entire life savings were wiped out within a matter of weeks or even days.

Tens of millions of homeowners lost their properties to foreclosure, and unemployment rose to levels not seen since the Great Depression of the 1930s.

Meantime, the vast majority of so-called "1-Percenters"—the wealthiest 1 percent of the population that holds the vast majority of the world's wealth—they continued to live in comfort. Some of them "shed tears" because their portfolios were now worth "mere" tens of millions of dollars, rather than hundreds of millions or even in the multiple billions.

Attention to the Super-Wealthy ~ Prepare to be Toppled

And, after all this, they—those super-wealthy people—they wonder why we're angry?

Unbelievable as this might sound, some of the super wealthy complain that we had the nerve and the gall to launch the national and international "Occupy" movement.

A huge percentage of the dim-witted super-wealthy strive to paint us a "loony birds" or "quacks" for having the gumption to protest.

To the contrary, a vast majority of us within the "occupy movement" are well educated, we're mad as hell, and we're not going to take their bullshit anymore.

We have risen up, and we will never be taken down until positive change erupts around the globe. We see millions upon millions of unemployed people—good, God-fearing, hard-working individuals left penniless due to the selfishness of 1-Percenters.

Our Unstoppable Movement Cannot be Halted

The Rich want us to shut up and to go away.

But now that our nests have been disrupted due to their greed, selfishness and greasy insider politics, we will never simply disappear unless they obliterate us.

We are the revolutionaries across the United States, Europe, Africa and Asia.

We, the revolutionaries, the occupiers, we have risen up across the Middle East against selfish regimes and dictatorships. We have put up with hogwash far too long.

Fed up with power politics, we have already toppled corrupt governments in such countries of Egypt and Libya.

And whether the 1-Percenters like this or not, let them know that more governments will fall, more corrupt politicians will soon face their ultimate demise.

CHAPTER 7
The Revolution Has Launched
~ Give Thanks

Let us give thanks that our anger has found a collective, unified effort.

Yes, we are thankful to the revolutions of yesterday, of today and those who will follow in our footsteps as we fight against corrupt governments and economic systems.

In a sense, we are much like those who fought the American Revolution against injustices of Great Britain, and the warriors of the French Revolution who rose up en masse in overthrowing the "let-the-eat-cake" aristocracy.

Indeed, those within the American 1-Percenters find themselves understandably afraid and even terrified—and they have every reason to feel this way.

Angry at what they have done to us and to our loved ones, we will carry forward with our "occupy efforts" until the necessary change comes about.

Our Collective Anger Swells

This collective anger shall continue to grow and swell, until such time as we achieve wisdom and discover the most efficient tactics to achieve our goals.

Every step of the way, the 1-Percenters undoubtedly will strive to have us portrayed in the collective public mindset as "mere, mindless, worthless turkeys."

The Rich will strive to portray us as fruitcakes, whiners, idiots, dope smokers, drug abusers and various other whacko malcontents.

This strategy on their part seems understandable. After all, the first and most logical step of any propaganda war is to demonize the enemy. Make us all look like fools, like idiots and as if we're jerks without any definable motive.

But the 1-Percenters need to be afraid, because we will overcome their shit-faced, overbearing strategies, their efforts to keep us under control.

Our Hearts Evolved into a Raging River

Our anger spills forth in endless rivers, as if the waters cascading across and under the Great Niagara Falls.

Our anger remains focused on the primary targets of Wall Street fat-cats who manipulate laws for their benefit and to the detriment of others.

Rage swells toward any and all politicians around the globe who put us, the 99 percent of the earth's population, into this whirlpool of economic destruction.

Surely, no one can deny our contempt for what has happened, to the point where collectively our effort has become a mighty, raging and roaring river.

Yet in the end the political waters shall flow, the torrents subsiding within placid lakes and oceans that come in the form of mutual respect.

CHAPTER 8
Who Are We?

We from among the 99 Percent within the Occupy Movement are a diverse, vibrant and passionate people.

Our masses range from the highly educated to the extremely ignorant.

Paradoxically, those supporting us or who join our relentless throngs include everyone from homeless people to even upper middle class and even a handful of Wealthy individuals.

From the very young to the extremely old, the ranks of our most passionate Occupy soldiers cover virtually every stratum of society—especially in the United States.

Many of those among us are poor communicators, speaking convoluted English while others within our ranks serve as masters at communicating their points of view on vital issues.

"Diversity" Reigns as Our Middle Name

We are senior citizens who lost their entire pensions due to the selfishness of big corporations, the Wall Street-backed financial industry and corrupt politicians.

Surveys consistently show that a huge percentage of us are young people, many in their 20s and early 30s. Lots of us among this age group or phase of personal growth never had a steady job, in many cases due to no fault of our own.

While many within this age group are highly educated, as an overall group we feel as if there is little to look forward to in matters of getting solid, reliable jobs.

We are the many unseen people, the formerly silent majority laid off by the tens of millions by giant, heartless, money-hungry corporations.

The strongest among us refuse to spend the rest of their lives toiling away for huge crappy companies that treat people as if expendable paper plates.

We Got Screwed "Playing by the Rules"

Huge percentages of our informal members always "played by the rules" before ultimately getting screwed by the evil, heartless Political Machine of 1-Percenters.

These new revolutionaries went to school, obeyed all laws and strived to get good jobs in hopes of moving up the ranks of corporate America. But a sharp reality hit.

Gone are the days when someone could earn a master's degree before landing a steady lifelong job. The era when one primary breadwinner could support a family has now been permanently relegated to the history books.

From the perspective of many of our most intellectual thinkers, the overall situation has been permanently turned "upside down"—destined to favor the 1-Percenters in perpetuity unless we effectively implement permanent change.

CHAPTER 9
Recognize our Enemies

Whether our Occupy Soldiers like to hear this or not, our enemies are a diverse lot. These adversaries hail from vastly differing segments of society.

The worst of our enemies are the Republican Party, and the Democratic Party—particularly extreme radicals within those philosophies.

Adding to our grief and woes, other failed political systems and ideologies include runaway capitalism, communism, racism, fascism, Marxism, and socialism.

Such systems are at their worst when carried to the extreme.

As if all these failed systems weren't already enough to cause unstoppable heartache, when mindless religious dogma comes to play—common sense goes out the window.

Nanny States vs. Ultra Wealthy

Ultra-liberal Democrats failed us by creating "nanny states" that are far too expensive to maintain, delving into the personal lives of our citizens. Worsening matters, these nincompoops sometimes have the audacity to pass legislation requiring that law-abiding, certified citizens and taxpayers pay the bill for the education and medical care of illegal aliens. Such idiocy has crippled the economy, putting taxpayers and law-abiding citizens under a seemingly inescapable mountain of debt.

Just as destructive, greedy, money-hungry and selfish ultra-conservatives in the Republican Party played integral roles enacting legislation that essentially gave the world's largest corporations carte blanche in running rip shod over the "little guy."

In essence, the Democrats have kept fighting to increase, solidify and maintain big government systems that are far too expensive to maintain. Meantime, mindless champions of the GOP lead a battle to minimize taxes for the very wealthy, using the lame and unsubstantiated argument that the "richest among us will enable the economy to grow through investment."

Yet such improvements never happened on either end of the political spectrum. Enabling the Wealthy 1-Percenters to escape taxes failed to generate the consistently promised economic benefits through the first decade of the 21st Century. All along, in a system promoted by liberals, the swelling size of national, state and local governments crushed the economies with excessive tax burdens.

All Political Systems Involve Greed

Within the United States and throughout the rest of the industrialized world, the push-pull political process pitting the wealthy against the poor and middle class swelled in favor of the 1-Percenters—a "snowball effect" that greatly picked up power and momentum through the 1990s and beyond.

All along, within virtually every culture including the former communist state of Russia and the semi-communist nation of China, greed played a vital role.

Ultimately, everyone was out for themselves, even as socialism and ultra-capitalistic systems failed.

The two-faced, phony national leaders of China emerged as some of the most corrupt 1-Percenters. While pretending to follow the most strict adherence to communism in the last half of the 20th Century, they steadily adopted an economic infrastructure that gave the benefited only the extreme elite within their society.

Occupiers Need to Face Difficult-to-Admit Truths

As disturbing as this might sound, it's true—the ranks of the Occupy Movement include fanatics within the Democratic and even the Republican parties.

Certainly, some of our members also have embraced other failed or lame-brained ideologies such as fascism, socialism and even Marxism.

For these people, the truth is "tough to take" and even "difficult to hear." In the end, however, all of them—each of us—

needs to face the fact that extremism has failed in virtually every political regard.

When all is said and done, a clear and distinct, undeniable truth comes into focus. Herein we must recognize that our nation and world have become mired an extremely difficult economic quagmire.

When smoke clogs the skies amid the heat of this Occupy War, we all must admit that a clear and distinct solution emerges.

CHAPTER 10
The Budget Deficit Crippled Our World

Whether they admit this or not, the Democratic Party and the Republican Party hold equal blame in creating the runaway U.S. budget deficit.

Public records give irrefutable proof that the budget of the United States swelled to nearly $15 trillion by late 2011.

Unless a viable solution is found, the crippling debt will impose a horrific financial burden on this generation and all subsequent generations throughout this century. These difficulties likely will hamper the ability of the USA to re-solidify the middle class.

As if pounding another nail onto the proverbial coffin of former middle-income earners, in October 2011 the U.S. Congressional Budget Office released data described by the Reuters News Service as showing that "in the last three decades, the United States has become a far more unequal nation."

The Rich Keep Getting Richer

"For the 1 Percent of the population with the highest income, average real after-tax household income grew by 275 percent between 1979 and 2007," according to the Congressional Budget Office, a non-partisan tax analysis and budget arm of the U.S. Congress.

By comparison, the report said, during the same period real after-tax household income grew by just under 40 percent among the lowest-income earners that comprise 60 percent of the population.

Such irrefutable statistics show that what many revolutionaries say rings true: "The rich just keep getting richer, and the poor and getting poorer."

This should come as highly frightening and disturbing news to the Wealthy 1-Percenters. That's because throughout recorded history in virtually all societies where the super-rich controlled a population for any lengthy period, the little guy has eventually revolted and thrown out their rulers.

These revolts have ranged from the French Revolution of the late 18th Century where regular folks overthrew and slaughtered the aristocracy, to the Russian Revolution of the early 20th Century when the masses destroyed the Tsarist aristocracy.

The Poor Keep Getting Poorer

The U.S. budget deficit of the early 21st Century clicked into full gear after Republicans used the treasury as a fascist tool to enable corporations to benefit from government construction, product sales and service projects, and for the purposes of nation-building.

The Democrats held just as much blame, eagerly bulking up a "government run amuck," a huge, cumbersome, unwieldy bureaucracy where inefficiency reigns supreme.

Both the liberals and the conservatives from among the Occupy Movement cringe at the mention of such tried-and-true facts.

Like little babies whining to get their way, each group—the Republican and Democratic parties—cry out while pointing an accusatory finger toward their political adversaries.

Rather than catering solely to the desires of special interest groups, these political combatants must fess up to their organizations' failings and work together to seek effective, workable solutions. Otherwise, whether any of us likes this or not, all-out anarchy will ensue.

CHAPTER 11
Gridlock Led to Anger

In the United States during the summer of 2011, the small-minded Republican Party and the whiny Democratic Party led to virtual gridlock in the U.S. Congress.

At a time when decisive, concise and cohesive action became paramount, each political party foolishly stood its ground—both holding to selfish political principles.

The anger among the U.S. electorate swelled almost the point of hate toward politicians, who insisted on clever hyperbole, name-calling and verbal trickery.

With the entire American economy on the line, rather than putting the interests of the general public first and foremost the political parties sucked up their warped ideologies.

During mid-summer, an August 4 deadline approached, opening the way for a possible U.S. government shutdown unless Congress made necessary tough decisions to raise the debt limit. Yet stubborn elected leaders stuck to their guns, waiting until the last minute to reach a deal.

We lost respect for Congress
Stupidly, failing to learn from their earlier lessons, these

shamefully inept Senators and congressional representatives agreed to a super-committee in both houses of Congress. These supposedly bi-partisan panels were given the responsibility of agreeing to necessary budget cuts by the Thanksgiving holidays.

And, unless an agreement could be reached, automatic and painful mandatory slashes in government expenditures were to kick into gear.

Once again sticking to their warped, demented economic philosophies, these political adversaries were on track to generate continued gridlock.

Their small-minded tactics, catering only to special interests served to ignite even more ire among those of 99-Percenters. Our elected leaders maintained partisan politics destined to "keep the little guy in his or her place," while catering to those who favor either big business or huge, overgrown governments.

Whether we want to admit this or not, once again those of us who favor either extreme Republican policies or harsh Democratic strategies collectively put the nation on course to lose any hope for long-term, workable solutions.

Political Parties Became Worthless

The Republic and Democrat lawmakers deserve our contempt for holding fast to their goofy, self-centered party lines while ignoring the needs of the people.

Essentially, everything came down to the fact that whether they knew this or not, members of Congress were igniting the initial flames of national "class warfare."

Generating the so-called perfect storm of political discontent, in the summer of 2011 the U.S. Congress pulled these shenanigans on the heels of the Arab Spring.

During the previous several months, curious North American

35

residents witnessed TV coverage of political uprisings across the Arab world. Continuing into the autumn, these uprisings resulted in the downfalls of 1-Percenter tyrants—especially Moammar Gadhafi of Libya, and Hosni Mubarak of Egypt.

Angered and pushed past the point of mere frustration, 99-Perceters took to the streets worldwide. These revolutionaries, many protesting publicly for the first time in their lives, rioted in the streets and in some instances launched bloody civil wars. That year marked the beginning of the increasingly powerful international Occupy Movement.

CHAPTER 12
Social Networks Became
Our Strategic Weapon

The Arab Spring launched the non-stop, highly effective use of Social Media technology in our national and international Occupy Movement.

With ever-increasing efficiency, Occupy Warriors have used Twitter, Facebook and other social network communications in organizing gatherings and strategies.

Lighting fast communications via laptops, personal computers, smart phones, cell phones and iPads cleared the way for social gatherings. Unwilling to remain complacent ever again, our international soldiers for change stepped up efforts to a higher degree by launching Websites and organizing regularly scheduled email updating systems.

The worried 1-Pecenters soon began saying that they looked forward to the natural death or fade-out of the Occupy Movement. Yet locked in "denial," these adversaries failed to realize that we would never willingly go away.

Our collective, relentless Social Networking systems kept us in tune with the steadily progressing need to organize more protests and "occupy" functions.

The 1-Percenters Need to Worry About Us

Rather than fade away as our enemies had hoped, those of us within the Occupy Movement are continuing to strengthen in numbers.

Thanks largely to modern communication technology, we have developed into the "bad dream" that the nervous and arrogant 1-Percenters have always worried about.

This increasingly intense war is more than merely a proverbial chess game, where one side emerges as a winner while the other loses—at least in the public mindset.

Filled with disgust at what has happened to us, and eager to effect positive change, our political firepower will only grow, solidify and strengthen. Indeed, our Occupy Armies have been and will continue to be a decisive force in modifying world history.

For many years, lots of social analysts have insisted that "all politics starts on the local level." The Social Networks have enabled us to make this happen at Occupy gatherings in cities and towns nationwide.

We Shall Peacefully Target Our Foes

During the coming months, years and decades as the Occupy Movement becomes increasingly formidable, our communications and planning efforts shall steadily improve.

Our detractors, especially those among the elite 1-Pecenters, will no longer mutter to themselves: "I cannot wait until this fades away." By that point, they shall realize that we are here to stay, and that we will never disappear on our own accord.

We might have been meek and downtrodden and used like serfs in the past, but the era of taking those of us within the 99-Percent for granted has gone forever thanks largely to the Social Networks.

As a result, we have an initial warning for those who would seek to permanently quell our effort. To those who want to pulverize us, always remember that we will find you and we will know who you are—as your names, and evil strategies become public knowledge.

In every case, we refuse to tolerate skullduggery, and those of you 1-Percenters who shall dare to smash our efforts shall find yourselves the targets of our peaceful discontent.

CHAPTER 13
Blood Will Flow in the Streets

During the initial years of our organized Occupy quest, the blood of our Warriors will continue to flow on the sidewalks and streets of the United States—and within other nations crammed with oppressed masses.

We organized ourselves as a peace-loving, non-violent movement, yet around the globe and within some segments of the United States militaries and police have attacked many within our innocent, unarmed Occupation Armies.

All along, every step of the way in our continued struggle, we embrace the peace-based teachings and strategies of such icons as Mohandas Gandhi of India and the Rev. Dr. Martin Luther King Jr. of the United States.

Despite our non-violent efforts, local police departments across the United States have already started to harass and to beat our peaceful Occupy Armies. Armed thugs employed by the military in the Syria have slaughtered literally dozens or hundreds of the revolting oppressed people.

Refusing to bow to those violent tactics, we on the domestic and international front continue to press forward partly in honor of our fallen comrades.

Armed Thugs Began Attacking our Peaceful Warriors

We remember and vividly recall images of Martin Luther King leading peace marches in the American South in the 1950s and 1960s, as police thugs whipped peaceful revolutionaries with batons and attacked them with firehouses.

Just as important, we remember Gandhi's non-violent struggles for peace as many of his warriors were slaughtered and harassed in India in the 1930s and 1940s.

Now, with the struggle more important than ever, we in the Occupy Movement have picked up the proverbial baton. This choice comes instinctively with little thought for our own protection as an overall group, because we know within our heart of hearts that decisive change must and should come.

Only through decisive action can that happen, and only through our own courage and strong-minded commitment can we bring about this necessary change.

Look For Us to Shake Things Up

Virtually every organization and army has its own "bad apples." The Occupy Movement is no exception in this regard.

Since individual people ultimately make their own choices, without any encouragement from us whatsoever, some within our ranks might resort to violence.

Such events likely will occur as a matter of their God-given right to self defense. Few people can tolerate baton whippings, tear gas attacks and rubber bullet barrages without eventually letting survival instincts motivate them to fight back.

Now and forevermore, we pray for those who might be injured during such bloody confrontations. Although we never seek to instigate such bloody brawls, we realize that those within the police state are merely doing their jobs—and just like any organization such as ours—those peace officers have their own share of bad apples.

Yet just because the authorities employ guns and bombs and video surveillance cameras, we shall not stray or back down from our efforts to peacefully disrupt the status quo. After all, things need to be shaken up once and for all.

CHAPTER 14
We Enjoyed a Wild Start

Like a newborn mustang in the open Western U.S. high desert, our Occupy Wall Street movement enjoyed a wild, fast start from the very beginning.

Initially launched in September 2011 by Adbusters, an activist group from Canada, we held our first organized gathering in Wall Street.

Intrigued, the mainstream news media and alternative communications systems soon started broadcasting our rallying cry: "We are the 99-Percenters." Within 21 days after the initial protests, at least 70 similar demonstrations were held in cities nationwide.

Today, we're not formally "controlled" by or permanently associated with any organization. No one owns us, or our name for that matter. Virtually all the other protests naturally and cohesively banded together under our Occupy Wall Street umbrella.

Amazingly, more than 900 similar demonstrations soon spread to other cities worldwide. Our ranks growing and solidifying as we collectively become strong, unbreakable and determined to implement positive, everlasting change.

All Political Parties "Suck"

All along, we remain cognizant of the fact that virtually all political parties and ideologies "suck"—everything from the Republicans and the Democrats, to communism, socialism, fascism, anarchy and dictatorships.

With all this clearly understood, we also acknowledge the indisputable fact that at least to some degree the overall Occupy Wall Street Movement "sucks" as well.

Added to this comes the longstanding fact that anyone who permanently latches on to a single political ideology or philosophy for all time is bound for inevitable disappointment. Nonetheless, now is the era when the Occupy Movement can and should make a permanent and positive mark on world history.

Otherwise, the 1-Percenters and the ludicrous politicians who embrace them will continue to trample over those of us in the 99-Percent majority.

To turn our backs on the vital Occupy Movement at this point would be to essentially slap the faces of all of our children, our grandchildren and their descendants.

Our Task Remains Formidable

Yes, it "sucks" to be misunderstood while serving in the Occupy Armies. It sucks to have to do the right and honorable thing, to struggle to overcome the many injustices imposed upon us by the heartless, oppressive and sometimes ignorant 1-Percent.

Those of us who champion the Occupy Movement often dislike the fact we find ourselves needing to spend our personal time and limited resources to join this valiant fight.

We know without any question whatsoever that our detractors are busy doing whatever they possibly can to discount us—to make us collectively and individually look like loons. Otherwise, our adversaries fear, the vast majority of the public will begin to embrace and to appreciate our efforts—perhaps joining us in this persistent struggle.

Even so, there can be no stopping our effort, especially as copies of this urgent and vital book spread rapid-fire around the world.

Our soldiers of Occupy justice stand tall in this regard, distrustful of any non-profit organization or public company that would dare to strive to occupy our formidable quest.

CHAPTER 15
Our Contempt Grew Unwieldy

The contempt among Occupy Soldiers for public officials swelled in size and scope when wimpy politicians failed to enact formidable regulations on the financial industry.

At least from the view of many Occupy advocates, the Obama administration weaseled out by failing to enact significant anti-predatory rules regulating Wall Street excesses.

Pushed to the point of anger, some officials in New York called for a national Day of Rage. The super-charged atmosphere finally began to intensify when the first Occupy Wall Street gathering kicked into full gear.

Meantime, the so-called Wall Street "fat cats" seemed to flaunt the protests, at least from the view of some of our peaceful revolutionaries.

In their various corporate filings and via media reports, huge multi-billion-dollar firms announced that big-company board chairman and CEOs were in some instances poised to receive record-high stock option bonuses.

In some instances, these totals reached hundreds of millions of dollars. All this occurred while unemployment remained at record-high levels in many regions, and home foreclosures clicked into gear at a rapid-fire pace.

Irrelevant Politicians Failed the People

During the initial six-week period after our sudden sizzling start-up launched into orbit, some protestors complained that U.S. President Barack Obama had become irrelevant in the quest, at least according to some news media accounts.

Hoping to seize an opportunity to stop our growth and to silence our growing discontent, many observers within the media started complaining that the Occupy movement lacked a specific agenda—let alone any vibrant focus.

Yes, those of us with fairly decent IQs found ourselves at least silently and privately admitting that "we suck"—just like all other political organizations. Be that as it may, at least we finally found ourselves with a platform of sorts.

Our detractors pointed out, and rightly so, that we had not yet found a way to address the many hardships and challenges facing today's 99-Percenters—particularly the young.

Chief among these objectives remained the need to find steady employment, to pay off student loans and to generate a solid, steady and reliable foundation for personal life.

Crony Capitalism Devastated the USA

Still, since the stage had finally been set, there could be no stopping our collective Occupy movement. Meantime, "crony capitalism" continued to prevail, in which huge companies depend on cozy relationships with government officials and politicians.

The increasingly popular film "Inside Job," narrated by Academy Award® winner Matt Damon, detailed how politicians appointed insiders within Wall Street and the elite educational infrastructure into key positions designed to regulate the financial industry.

Amid the initial upheaval or "birthing pangs" experienced during initial stages of the Occupy Movement, some media analysts desperately strived to portray us as ultra-liberal or "Democrat whacko" proponents.

Yet those of us within this new struggle realized and admitted to the fact that the "sucking" Democrat Party holds just as much of the blame for fostering or generating the USA's financial mess as the heartless GOP.

CHAPTER 16
Corruption Oozes from Wall Street

Any initial problems in organizing our movement failed to obliterate or hide the fact that corruption oozes from almost every core of the Wall Street infrastructure.

Shady or suspect political ties between those in the highest ranks of the corporate and stock trading industries ensure that the rich get richer while the poor get screwed.

A vast majority of our initial Occupy Members agreed that these wrongdoings seemed an obvious target for change.

However, according to at least some news reports, the initial ranks within our Occupy Movement broke into two segments.

Those wishing to focus on the inequitable distribution of wealth reportedly diverged from participants who wanted the movement to grow through the spectacle of occupying public places.

Adding to our initial image as "wimpy," at least from the perspective of some pontificators, organizers who fashioned themselves as Occupy leaders either failed or refused to issue any list of specific demands.

Weakness permeated our embryonic stage

Just like almost every civil war or essential societal revolution from throughout history, our Occupy Movement lacked cohesiveness during its embryonic stage. Some insiders or participants insisted that issuing demands should never have been considered.

Instead, from their view, the mere process of amassing in Occupy protests at least for the time being gave people as sense of continuity—of being in the same community.

Meantime, some opinions emerged that the protestors needed to make their feelings known via public protests and rallies. Such open displays of collective anger never would have been necessary if politicians had done their job in the first place by enacting much-needed legislation.

Even so, various political commentators strived to portray all this essentially as the weakness of liberal goofballs. Many of these pot shots got fired from pontificators from the far right who support the ultra-Wealthy 1-Percenters.

These made for crafty, quickie sound bites on conservative news reports such as "The O'Reilly Factor" starring Bill O'Reilly on the Fox News Network.

Irresponsible TV Commentators Failed the USA

Shamefully, performing a disservice to sound, respectable journalists everywhere, at one point O'Reilly had a film crew interview a single Occupy protestor. Of course, that particular individual never represented our entire movement.

Nonetheless, palming this guy off as if he was an official spokesman for the Occupy Movement, O'Reilly's film crew captured images of the man spouting nonsense about Wall Street essentially being evil—because, as the guy on the street ignorantly claimed, it's "controlled by Jews."

O'Reilly correctly pointed out that the man's statements were anti-Semitic and over-the-top. Yet this arrogant TV commentator then proceeded to indicate essentially that these are the kinds of people or philosophies that permeate the Occupy movement.

Striving to achieve ratings boosts and to incite anger among viewers and listeners, conservative TV and radio hosts strived to give little specific in-depth detail about those within the Occupy Armies—other than to portray them as over-the-top liberals.

All along, however, numerous so-called conservative individuals also joined our ranks, some of them as eager as the rest of us to eradicate our government of snotty policies that favor only the super Wealthy.

CHAPTER 17
Let the Word Go Forth ~ We Will Persist

The blood of peaceful Occupy Soldiers began to flow on the streets of the United States in October 2011.

Overzealous police in Oakland, California, and in New York City attacked our innocent, unarmed and strong-willed protestors. Many of us within the Occupy movement realized that those attacks marked the beginning of our physical plight.

Those of us who remained cognizant of history realized that the worst was yet to come. We knew from that point that in the coming months and years our peaceful crusaders would become the target of government harassment.

In almost every society where the poor have risen up against the elite Wealthy, blood has been shed by the downtrodden. Communists slaughtered innocent people by the hundreds of thousands or even the millions in the 1920s and 1930s, primarily under Stalin's Russia regime.

Similar but far more horrific patterns played out when the Nazis slaughtered many millions of Jewish people during the German Third Reich of the 1930s and 1940s. Some journalists and social experts have estimated that from 1.7 million to 2.5 million people died under the Cambodian regime of Pol Pot during the late 1970s.

The 1-Percenters Seek to Annihilate Our Revolutionaries

Those of us within the Occupy Movement who remain fully cognizant of world history fully realize that at least some 1-Percenters will eagerly seek to eradicate and totally eliminate any and all of us who would dare to protest.

When that phase clicks into full gear, the Super Wealthy and their cronies in the media will seek to characterize us in the general media as "flakes" and "whacko."

Our Occupy Armies of peaceful protestors should anticipate such untruthful and conniving propaganda. Amid these struggles, people from around the world should expect and fully anticipate Warriors for the State to beat our innocent masses with batons. Tear gas attacks instigated by police coupled with the firing of rubber bullets became our initial fears.

The overzealous police and reckless officials in Oakland, California, served as cronies for the 1-Percenters when they attacked an Iraq War veteran from the United States who had joined our protests. Occupy Armies at organized gatherings in hundreds of cities worldwide immediately saw this as a signal that physical attacks on us would intensify. Our call for victory intensified.

Police and the Military Mobilized Against Us

Many of us knew without any shadow of a doubt that as our overall movement pressed forward, local, state and national governments would mobilize police and military units to quell or break up our peaceful gatherings.

Striving to enrage the overall public against us, officials started spreading propaganda indicating our protests were causing governments hundreds of millions of dollars. This nonsense only served to increase the anger among some of our staunchest and most loyal advocates.

From cities across Europe to communities throughout Asia and the United States, local Occupy Movement organizers helped organize their own gatherings.

Yes, what started out as a local gathering in the New York City area had suddenly swelled into a nationwide and international movement.

Once the wheels of change began, there could be no stopping our collective force. The more those public officials, supported by 1-Percenters, balked at our peaceful gatherings, the more defiant and obstinate we became.

CHAPTER 18
Our Members Would Die by the Millions

Hundreds of thousands or even millions of our Occupy Warrior bodies will be bulldozed into mass graves, at least if some 1-Percenters have their way.

These are the distinct worries of some of our most learned members, fully aware that some of the world's Wealthiest people would never publicly disclose such wretched plans. Our Soldiers need to always remain fully cognizant that at least a small percentage of the Super Wealthy has consistently shown such violent tendencies.

As a result, those of us who might be naïve about such realities need to fully grasp these facts. If and when the overall world economy continues to crumble, as some of us fear, class warfare will erupt around the globe—particularly within the United States.

Remember, we refuse to condone violence of any kind. Yet when and if basic, necessary commodities such as food become scarce, street-to-street and hand-to-hand combat is likely to erupt across the United States.

As radical as such an outcome might sound, remember that such shortages remain a distinct possibility. A so-called "perfect storm" could easily form, especially if the overall economy fails to kick into full gear as worldwide food shortages swell in scope and severity. Many of us in the U.S. culture fail to realize that food riots already started erupting across numerous nations in 2010 and into early 2011.

Many People Anticipate Anarchy Within the United States
Those of us lacking funds for food, shelter and weapons likely will become the initial targets, especially when and if such individuals join our ranks at peaceful gatherings.

Constant gunfire from government soldiers that riddled and massacred protesting civilians in Syria likely marked just the beginning of such attacks worldwide.

Early on, Occupy Soldiers in small and mid-size communities and huge cities across the United States need to remain wary of such increased tension.

At some point, many of us fear, the U.S. government—

primarily supported by corrupt lobbyists and high-powered politicians supported by the Super Wealthy—is likely to shut down cell phone communication and even Facebook or Twitter access. During initial weeks of the Egypt uprising, authorities in that nation tried similar tactics.

Carrying such worries a step further, also keep in mind that the U.S. government has stepped up secretive, wide-scale surveillance of our own citizenry. At this juncture, the very government that we pay to protect us is in the process of eavesdropping on private conversations of its own citizens without court-ordered warrants, and also spying on our emails.

The Government Targeted All of Us for Surveillance

The many among our Occupy Movement ranks who passionately love the United States find such surveillance as an extreme disappointment.

At the same time, lots of us realize and fully appreciate the fact that the nation's Defense Department has an urgent need to find, monitor, hunt and destroy terrorists who would seek to harm the United States.

In the wake of the world population's recent surge past the 7 billion mark, the United States and the international community face more danger than ever before. Many of us within the Occupy Movement recognize these harsh realities. We embrace the pressing need to address these problems.

When considered on a worldwide scale, 6.93 billion people are oppressed, poor and struggling to survive. Assuming such calculations are on the mark that means a mere 70 million people control the fate of nearly 7 billion individuals.

Sadly, many of us within the Occupy Movement know full

well from history that numerous political strategies all designed to "spread the wealth" including Socialism, Marxism and Communism all are dismal failures—especially when taken to the extreme.

CHAPTER 19
Where Can You Run? And, Where Can You Hide?

Are you in denial of the pain that lurks for us all just around the corner?

Just look at the television and see the people rioting, protesting and struggling to survive all around the world. Rather than look the other way, many of us within the Occupy Movement see the problems straight ahead facing us all.

Unlike many of the 1-Percenters, we realize that educators, police departments, firefighters and other government services lack adequate funding.

Perhaps even more important, we see and acknowledge the fact that the disparity between the very rich and the extremely poor is continuing to widen.

Besides merely feeling anger, we know full well that the environment continues to deteriorate to extremely dangerous levels due to mankind's ignorance and selfishness.

Extreme Danger Faces the 99-Percenters

Lots of us within the Occupy Armies feel as though the 1-Percenters prefer to view the world through rose-tinted glasses. Living in the lap of luxury, fancy dinners and mansions, the vast majority of the Wealthy either refuse to accept or to acknowledge that our environment is being irrefutably damaged. Even worse, these same individuals either ignore or refuse to care about the extensive plight of the extremely poor.

Ultimately, this "survivor mentality" on the part of the Super Wealthy has led to the moral degradation of our society.

Herein springs forth a disturbing truth that has repeated itself consistently throughout history. Each and every society that lost its moral focus crumbled, from the Romans Empire to the Mongolian Empire, plus the Nazi regime.

Now, during the current era, whether those of us within the Occupy Movement like to say this or not, the Wealthy 1-Percent now finds itself on the precipice of ultimate change—and an eventual awakening due largely to its own ethical failings.

Snot-nosed Politicians Emerged as Weak

Those of us who live in mud shacks, those of us who are homeless on the streets of America and those of us who have lost our houses to foreclosure know the heartache. We are tired, we are sapped of energy and we have been beaten down by our corrupt government, lobbyists and corporations.

Yet, somehow we find ourselves strong, strengthened by this Occupy Movement. Yes, this can't be said enough, "we suck" just like all political systems and ideologies do.

But at least by amassing in throngs, we now have true "hope" in the actual sense of the word. This is not corny or vote-for-me hope such as that spouted by ambitious, self-serving politicians who never came even close to delivering.

Individually and collectively, many of us within the Occupy Movement realized early on in this quest that many difficulties faced us in the near future.

We realized that through no fault of our own, class warfare could very well erupt within our American homeland. Remember, what we saw on the disturbing nightly news reports could very well emerge as the mere seed of swelling, widespread violence.

CHAPTER 20
Geniuses Know When to Escape

Throughout history some of the world's greatest geniuses have seized opportunities to flee their homelands, rather than face brutal, totalitarian regimes.

Key among these luminaries who saw the proverbial "writing on the wall" early on was the genius Albert Einstein. Facing up to the truth of looming, ever-growing dangers within Nazi Germany, he left Europe for the United States in the 1930s. Within the next decade millions of other Jews were slaughtered by the Third Reich.

Some of us within the Occupy Movement fear that the United States now faces just such a precipice. Amid continued and persistent economic collapse, the USA seemed on the verge of horrific internal strife—at least from the view of some observers.

Many within the Occupy Movement sense a similar national downfall, although we desperately love this country and the supposed freedoms that have been afforded to us.

Yet in the eyes of many observers, from "sea to shining sea" America seems as if teetering on the precipice of collapse on an economic and governmental basis.

We Should Avoid Treason

A glimpse of the nightly TV news or at the few remaining newspapers with any semblance of respectability reveals a nation on the verge of potential collapse.

In the United States, any act of treason or a designed plan or conspiracy to overthrow the national government is a felony. Under the 1917 Espionage Act and the 1798 Alien and Sedition Acts, those who attempt to overthrow the U.S. government face severe penalties. Even the most strident among the Occupy Army never would suggest or encourage such unlawful actions.

Even so, the economic plight and widespread difficulties facing the USA lead many of us to fear what once seemed unthinkable.

Could severe food shortages, indifference by the Wealthy 1-Percent and the widening disparity among economic classes lead to all-out anarchy within the United States? Will our weak-willed politicians and corrupt lobbyists result in a society where the vast majority of citizens either refuse or fail to recognize the authority of our government?

Perhaps just as frightening, would such a loss of respect for our leaders and our rules lead to lawlessness and political disorder? When and if that occurs, how will our federal and local governments respond? Could officials quell such outbursts, and restore peace?

Never Depend on Our Inept Government

Proving once again what has prevailed throughout history, that all governments are inherently inept, the USA failed to respond in a timely, effective manner to the Katrina Hurricane disaster in New Orleans and to many other floods and tornadoes since then.

Amid the deadly Katrina-caused flooding in 2005, thousands of people were shown on nationwide TV as they pleaded for help at the Louisiana Superdome. Sadly, our government proved inept and inadequate at assisting and saving the very people that it's sworn to protect.

Considering that this occurred on a relatively regional basis, think of what the outcome would be like if a horrific societal outburst occurred on a nationwide basis.

With little doubt, many of the most ardent Occupy Soldiers strongly believe that our national, state and local governments would be woefully inadequate at helping citizens during widespread, horrific disasters.

An overriding, significant fear emerges. When and if lawlessness erupts within almost every town and street in the USA, how can we survive? What will become of our nation, and who can we look to for leadership other than the Wealthy 1-Percenters?

CHAPTER 21
View This Revolution as Necessary

"Every generation needs a revolution," said Thomas Jefferson, author of the Declaration of Independence and the third president of the United States.

While such statements might sound romantic to some people, lots of us within the Occupy Movement know fully well and respect the fact that difficult trials lie ahead.

Just like General George Washington, the first president of the United States, many of us within the Occupy Armies appreciate the need to remain as emotionally strong and as vigorous as possible amid the peak of the coming political battles.

Meantime, lots of our initial adversaries today—particularly cronies supported by the 1-Percenters—complain that "the Occupy Movement lacks any focus" and that those "protestors don't have any plan or a list of demands."

Well, that may be true at least to some degree at the early onset of this urgent quest. Yet keep in mind that our nation's founding fathers also lacked a distinct, clear list of definable objectives during early and mid-level stages of the American Revolution.

Keep in mind that the United States Constitution was not adopted until September 1787, more than 11 years after the Declaration of Independence was ratified. The Constitution was finally authorized four years after the end of the 8-year-long American Revolutionary War.

And, the U.S. Bill of Rights, particularly the initial amendments to the Constitution, did not come until 1789—two years after the U.S. government was formally organized.

Our Detractors Can Eat Fresh Poop

With history as our guiding post, those of us who cherish the Occupy Movement can tell our most ardent detractors to "eat poop" when they criticize us for not having a plan or a clear, distinct list of specific grievances.

Worsening matters, lots of our detractors—especially small-minded conservative talk show hosts—spout off misinformation about our apparent demands.

In some instances, these pontificators have claimed that we would like to essentially "steal from the rich" in order to give to the poor.

Under this scenario, we supposedly demand that government hammer out a system where the 20 percent of the poorest among us get handed essentially "free cash, essentially for doing nothing to earn such incomes."

Well, first off, nothing could be further from the truth. We have made no such demands. Even so, in an effort to pump up their radio or TV ratings, these jerks have proven themselves as enemies of everything that's good and right about America.

Overly eager to pull off such deceptions, in some instances these morons have pulled lists of possible demands that some of our members wrote independently on blogs—listing their own personal opinions. The propagandists within the media subsequently spouted off these goals, incorrectly announcing to the world that these objectives were our official, formalized grievances.

Ignore the "Weenie Analysts"

Those of us dead-set on continuing with this vital, urgent and necessary revolution need to steer clear of such nincompoops— those who babble in the media, striving to stir up rage in order to generate big ratings.

Rather than communicating constructively in an effort to resolve issues, some of our most popular detractors choose to fan the flames of public discontent.

Reckless political statements have spewed from the mouths of such supposed, undeserved luminaries as conservative talk radio host Rush Limbaugh, and the horribly arrogant Bill O'Reilly of the Fox News Television Network. Political dope-heads such as these choose to fan the flames of public discontent, rather than to talk reasonably about issues that impact our entire nation.

Just as guilty of reckless political statements are the pinheads on the other side of the spectrum, especially some of the morons in anchor chairs at the ultra-liberal MSNBC-TV cable network. Also eager to pump up reviews, some of these liberal bubbleheads have wrongly strived to portray our moment as championing the liberal cause.

Well, nothing could be further from the truth, particularly from the point of view of some Occupy Movement revolutionaries who see both the Republican and Democratic parties as dismal failures—both corrupt, each in the pocket of big business, lobbyists and the Wealthy 1-Percenters.

CHAPTER 22
The Tea Party Movement Sucks Donkey Dung

Like all political organization, we in the Occupy Movement admit that we "suck." But far worse than that, the Tea Party Movement stinks to the point of being evil.

You see, anything taken or acted in the extreme is "evil." For instance, excessive use of drugs, far too much booze, and non-stop gambling become wicked and destructive. Anything in extreme, excessive amounts—even marijuana, whether some of us choose to admit this or not—results in extremely painful and highly destructive situations.

The Tea Party, in all its various sour forms and flavors, is just as bad, pernicious and destructive as communism, socialism and even pornography. At its core, the Tea Party is a wicked, vile organization that covets primarily the needs of the very wealthy.

For anyone unfamiliar with the Tea Party, let's just say that the organization wants to slash government to the bare bones—cutting away all the vital and necessary meat of the American bureaucracy.

Of course, all governments suck, so at least the Tea Party is correct in this regard. Be that as it may, governments are a necessary evil, vital in order to help implement necessary checks and balances—all essential in keeping the 1-Percenters at bay, hopefully positioned where they can cause the least damage possible upon the poor.

Ignore Tea Party Hogwash

The Tea Party would seek to hypnotize the entire public, striving to convince us to believe that no military is necessary to protect our national interests.

We're supposed to swallow the Tea Party's endless hogwash, their harsh criticisms of some political efforts to help certain homeowners who experienced mortgage foreclosures to refinance.

Rather than cite weak governmental policies that enabled the 1-Percenters to run amok over the finance industry, many Tea Party advocates sought to portray people who lost their homes to foreclosure as weak, incompetent or exhibiting "bad behavior."

Under this warped line of thinking, the Tea Party Movement would have us all believe the that people left homeless, unemployed or otherwise financially devastated by the Great Recession were to blame—not the 1-Percenters who intentionally issued "bad loans."

Predictably, public opinion polls revealed that a majority of Tea Party advocates were wealthy people over age 45, rather than young parents struggling to make ends meet. Sticking to their guns like rowdy kindergarteners at recess, this despicable organization cajoled several presidential candidates to refrain from tax increases of any kind whatsoever.

What is a Political Ass-Kisser?

Although most Occupy Movement supporters never openly or wantonly hate anyone, lots of us find ourselves repulsed by butt-suckers like political candidates that agreed to "paint themselves into a corner" in order to win Tea Party support.

"Meager souls, mystics and revolutionaries may promise to refashion the world in accordance with their dreams—but evil remains, and so long as it lurks in the secret places of the heart, utopia is only the shadow of a dream," said Nathaniel Hawthorne, a 20th Century American short story writer and novelist.

Indeed, whether they realize this or not, many Tea Party advocates are short-sighted, watching out for the interests of a miniscule section of society. In doing so, these individuals have turned their backs on the Golden Rule taught by Jesus Christ and some of the other great spiritual figures of all time.

Yes, the Tea Party members would tell us: "Let's wipe out programs that help the poorest among us—let them starve, or fend for themselves. Let them eat cake."

Well, let the word go forth from this point forward, that many of us within the Occupy Movement choose to stand tall on a higher, more righteous and honorable ground. Instead of turning our backs on our brothers, our fellow men and women, we choose love—because love conquers all.

CHAPTER 23
The Wealthy ~ Who are They?

Unlike during the 18th Century, 19th Century and the early part of the 20th Century, the bulk of today's mega-wealthy people are not descendants of aristocracy.

Surveys and public census data in recent decades consistently shows that the vast majority of today's Super Rich are board members of major corporations, real estate tycoons and hedge fund managers or operators.

For the most part, these individuals used their greasy business connections, back-room deals and deceptive shenanigans to achieve loads of stock and cash.

A significant part of this process involves controlling our government, primarily via campaign donations totaling tens of millions of dollars. This process ultimately puts in place selfish politicians who enact rules, regulations and taxes designed to screw the average American—particularly anyone "unlucky" enough not to sit on corporate boards.

Huge corporations also zip straight into this greasy muck, championing legislation designed to pump up stockholder value while poking the average American up the ass.

Rich People Own our Government

"I don't mind you being rich—but I mind you buying our government," said a protest sign carried by one of our Occupy Warriors, summing up what many of us feel.

With literally hundreds of millions of dollars, or perhaps billions, primarily from corporations and the mega-wealthy, going toward political campaigns the average person gets left in the proverbial gutter of the American economy like discarded trash.

As a prime example, consider the corrupt intermingling of the giant General Electric Co., and our incompetent, corporate-owned government. Although one of the world's largest companies and based in the United States, during calendar year 2010 GE legally avoided paying even a single cent in taxes to the U.S. government.

Showing additional contempt for the American public, a top GE executive, Jeffrey R. Immelt, was appointed by President Obama to head a panel assigned with the task of creating jobs in the United States—the President's Economic Recovery Advisory Board—in February 2009.

Shockingly, from the view of many Occupy Movement supporters, in July 2011 General Electric announced that its X-ray division would be moved to China from Wisconsin. Once again, the Obama administration and Corporate America thumbed its nose at the U.S. public, essentially saying to us all: "You people are dog shit."

Republicans and Democrats Kiss Major Ass

Like the board members and CEOs at other major U.S.

corporations, Immelt pulled in many millions of dollars in annual salary plus lucrative stock options.

Weak-kneed, shifty and gutless politicians such as Obama, U.S. House Speaker John Boehner, a Republican, and U.S. Senate Democratic Majority Leader Harry Reid sucked in huge campaign donations from top corporations and Wall Street fat cats.

In the process Corporate America and the 1-Percenters continued to achieve their runaway, unchecked goal of solidifying the whims and demands of big-money special interest organizations.

Worsening an already horrible situation, shortly after taking office in early 2009 the wimpy Obama of the Democratic Party appointed Wall Street insiders—the same type of clowns that caused the Great Recession—to regulate the U.S. finance industry.

At the time, less than five months after the sharp downward stock market trend began in September 2008, cronies from both sides of the political aisle generally applauded Obama's scum-sucking appointments. Overall, the president's selections were tantamount to choosing crafty, hungry foxes to guard a chicken pen.

Politicians Live in Luxury

Well-ensconced in their lives of luxury, cushy political salaries and basking in the media limelight, Democrats like Obama and Republicans like Pennsylvania Governor Christopher James "Chris" Christie send their children to cushy private schools.

Rich politicians such as these from both sides of the political aisle join the extremely Wealthy in positioning themselves away from the 99-Percent in society.

Our children attend under-funded public schools, where underpaid teachers do their best in less-than-ideal conditions. Meantime, the offspring of the slimiest politicians and the

67

extremely rich get sheltered from such hardships and daily challenges.

Whenever anyone dares to question politicians such as Christie from proposing cuts to public education—while sending their own kids to cushy, extremely expensive private schools, the politicians yell back: "How dare you attack my family!"

Although perceived as a darling by many Republicans who had lobbied Christie to run for president due to his direct, tough-talking style, the Pennsylvania governor is essentially a mirror image of Obama in many regards. Both of them are weenies, the same kind of cheap talkers who support the agendas of wealthy contributors.

CHAPTER 24
The Wealthy Use Politicians and Lobbyists as Puppets

Owned by the Super Wealthy and the world's largest corporations, the highest-level politicians across America and in many other nations serve as puppets or marionettes.

High-paid lobbyists perform a similar role, all of them moving to the beck and call of huge campaign contributors or their crafty employers.

For each corrupt person involved, everything comes down to greed. The lust for money, power and sometimes political fame rules the day—mostly while blatantly ignoring the needs, desires and goals of the large majority of regular Americans.

Yes, so-called liberty has its definite drawbacks. Whether

we like to admit this or not, especially among those of us in the Occupy Movement, the system is set up and solidified to benefit only the rich and politically powerful.

The First Amendment to the U.S. Constitution guarantees us "freedom of speech," yet amid our initial protests we the Occupy Soldiers must admit to ourselves that elected leaders are likely to listen only to those who have huge financial caches. The age-old phrase that "money talks while poverty falls upon deaf ears" still rings true.

So, under this line of thinking, admitting the facts, we Occupiers can yell on street corners all we want, march with protest signs, amass at rallies to make fantastic speeches to one another—and work to educate the general public about this problem.

Still, we always remain cognizant that no significant changes can or will occur, until such time as we have stockpiles of money in order to spark necessary change.

Lobbying permeates an aura of evil

The lobbying system used within the United States permeates the essence of evil, because this extreme process eliminates the needs and desires of "regular folks."

An eruption of questionable ethics crosses the line between healthy government and all-out dysfunction, diving deep into the realm of immorality due to the overall absence of any significant oversight that looks out for the so-called little guy.

Huge masses of lobbyists representing everything from the auto insurance industry to drug manufacturers benefit from continual access to national lawmakers.

As a result, industries such as the conglomerate drug producers, often called "Big Pharma," enact predatory laws that enable them to gouge consumers. Per-pill prices sometimes skyrocket for certain pharmaceuticals, thereby making vital and sometimes life-saving prescriptions unavailable to many desperate consumers.

Worsening matters, stringent regulations and requirements often insisted upon by lobbyists and huge contributors to political campaigns often mandate that insurmountable paperwork and insurance requirements be imposed upon new entrepreneurs. This process, in turn, helps ensure that certain huge companies never face serious, significant competition.

Corporate America Generates Hogwash

Significant power struggles erupt within the realm of lobbyists, with Wealthy people, huge companies or organizations that dole out the largest donations often getting what they want from government.

Once again, the poor and former middle-class Americans get left with slim pickings, struggling to make ends meet amid increasingly difficult economic times.

Among perennially positive U.S. President Ronald Reagan's most heralded statements in the 1980s was: "Government is not the solution to the problem; government is the problem."

More precisely, many of us in the Occupy Movement might say during the first quarter of the 21st Century that "Lobbyists and warped political campaign laws make our government and our politicians corrupt, clearing a pathway for the 1-Percenters to hog most of the wealth, own our government and squeeze the 99-Percent of our population."

The First Amendment of the U.S. Constitution gives the people the "right to petition" our government. However, since politicians are puppets within the pockets of the Wealthy and Corporate America, any petitions issued by us 99-Percenters likely will fall on deaf ears among powerbrokers unless we legally change our legislative system.

CHAPTER 25
1-Percenters Squeeze Out the Unions

The lobbyists and politicians have worked hard to grab labor unions by the groin, doing everything possible to castrate or denigrate working class Americans—both male and female.

Labor unions that have represented teachers, police officers and factory workers have seen drastic cutbacks in their ability to engage in collective bargaining. As a result, wages, benefits and working conditions for the 99-Percenters have dwindled.

Some economists, politicians and representatives for 1-Percenters might argue that those greedy labor organizations have contributed greatly to the nation's economic woes.

Government pensions earned by or demanded from certain public sector workers have been blamed for generating crippling tax rates and stifling business, while average taxpayers aren't even represented by unions.

Meantime, through their cronies the lobbyists, certain

politicians and selfish political organizations, the 1-Percenters and Corporate America strive to demonize labor unions. Experts at linguistic hogwash, some of these anti-worker propagandists call some regions "right-to-work states," which actually designates areas where Fascist legislation makes an ideal climate for Big Business and the Wealthy to bombard unions—squeezing all of us regular people into a life of poverty.

Strike an ideal balance

Like any political organization or economic philosophy, labor unions have the distinct and overriding possibility of "sucking big time"—just like all the other scum within our society.

Remember, lots of us within the Occupy Movement fervently believe that anything in excess is "evil, wicked or at least highly ineffective." When used in extreme amounts, labor unions can drag down vital industries, making profitability almost impossible.

In fact, some cronies of the 1-Percenters argue—and rightly so—that organized labor played a big role in motivating Corporate America to move millions of jobs overseas.

On the flip side of the same coin, however, labor unions also have played a vital, necessary and urgent role in sticking up for the rights, working conditions and compensation efforts of the American worker.

A through analysis of the overall situation leads many of us Occupy Soldiers to believe that both the Lobbyist-Politician Coalition and Organized Labor have a distinct possibility for evil and amazingly for "good" as well under the right conditions.

Weakness abounds in the political realm

The USA has a long, extensive and diverse history of organized labor unions. Politicians in the pockets of 1-Percenters used weakness and corruption within unions as an excuse in enacting 1947 federal legislation that weakened unions, the Taft-Hartley Act. Meantime, historians tell us that unions played a significant role in molding modern liberalism in the United States.

From the perspective of some political scientists, for the most part unions were favored by people of liberal or Democratic preferences, while conservatives or those in the Republican faction favored anti-union, Big Business strategies.

When taken to the extreme, both philosophies can and often do result in severe problems for society. Major setbacks or long-term stumbling blocks can range from excessive tax burdens necessary to augment public sector retirements, to Big Business squeezing out unions in order to essentially suck the blood out of the working class.

Those of us within the Occupy Movement with a clear vision of these diverging and opposing perspectives know that significantly favoring either could result in big-time hassles for all of society.

A world-famous quotation credited to Patrick Henry when addressing the Virginia House of Burgess in 1775 proclaims: "Give me liberty or give me death." To those of us seeking a common-sense balance between today's labor movements, Big Business and government bureaucracy, the quote should echo: "Give us unions, industry and government that sucks as little as possible."

CHAPTER 26
Where are the 1-Percenters Hiding?

Since our Occupy Movement suddenly blossomed on a widespread scale, where have all the Mega-Wealthy people gone?

Goodness knows we never see these people proudly standing on street corners or going on TV programs to say: "I'm a 1-Percenter, and I'm proud of it because I've profited by screwing the little guy—out of their jobs and out of their homes."

But why? What motivates such people to hide out? Where and how might they stand tall, speaking proudly of their motivations and strategies for "sticking it to" us 99-Percenters?

Quite honestly, these cowardly individuals are hiding out, never discussing the specific issues in expansive public forums for the most part and owning up to their individual roles in robbing the general public blind.

Instead of handling these dirty, cumbersome chores as an overall group the Mega Wealthy and the 1-Percenters prefer to have their cronies, politicians, lobbyists, activist organizations and propaganda machines handle all such dirty work.

Fluff Journalism Harmed our Cause

Shortly after the Occupy Movement began some billionaires started getting sweet-sugary attention—the type of ideal propaganda that the 1-Percenters crave.

Four billionaires appeared a ABC-TV "20/20" episode hosted by none other than Barbara Walters, who herself was born into a mega-wealthy family.

Rather than engage in hard-nose, informative and controversial interviews with these privileged individuals, Walters engaged in cream puff-style interactions possibly designed to make the billionaires look like Saints sent the earth by the Hand of God.

Paul Mitchell hair products founder and Patron Spirits owner John Paul DeJoria received just as many of Walter's softball questions as Lynn Tilton of Patriarch Partners. Getting just as much candy-coated coverage on the program were Zappos CEO Tony Hsieh, and Cirque du Soleil founder Guy Laliberte.

Could possible reasons for this sugary coverage emerge, when considering that the ABC Television Network is owned by one of the world's largest super-conglomerates, the Walt Disney Company?

One of the largest companies in the world, this firm is so huge that it's among the 30 publicly traded firms that collectively comprise the Dow Jones Industrial Average—commonly referred to as simply the "Dow." With gross revenues at $38 billion in fiscal 2010, perhaps the fat cats in Disney's corporate offices wanted to refrain from upsetting the proverbial apple cart in clearing the way for Walter's blatant propaganda.

More Creepy Propaganda Spread

Another possible propaganda tool designed to make the Stinking Wealthy look like angels in the eyes of the public was CBS-TV's "Undercover Boss" program.

During this peachy show's initial run in the 2009-2010 season, top executives at a diverse range of conglomerates were shown shamelessly passing out gifts such as college scholarships or all-expenses-paid vacations to their frontline workers.

The average per-episode premier program viewer total for the period reached a whopping 17.7 million. This marked a major grand slam for the broadcaster, CBS Corporation, a major firm traded on the New York Stock Exchange with $14 billion in annual gross revenue.

Apparently tickled pink by their propaganda success from "Undercover Boss," CBS has announced that it will air an undisclosed number of new episodes in the winter of 2012.

According to at least some published reports, CBS fat cat and executive chairman Sumner Redstone has a net work of less than $3.8 billion. At Disney, Robert A. "Bob" Iger earned $29 million in 2009, including his base salary and stock options.

CHAPTER 27
The Corporate-owned Media Distorted
Our Message

Fired up, in a concerted effort to make the Occupy Movement look like a "goofball operation," news media conglomerates controlled by billionaires issued non-stop "stories" portraying our urgent mission as foolish and aimless.

Key among these was News Corporation, owner of the "Wall Street Journal" newspaper, and the Fox News Network.

Boasting gross annual revenues of $33 billion, this mega-corporation sent its proverbial attack dogs in the form of journalists and TV analysts.

A disservice to the journalism profession and failing all Americans, these programs and stories fueled the flames of public discontent, instilling anger against Occupiers—incorrectly for the most part portraying us as ignorant street warriors without definite goals.

The anti-American sentiment of Bill O'Reilly and Sean

Hannity, hosts of separate Fox News Network shows, work diligently to collectively paint all of us as scumbags.

Corruption Permeates the Conservative Mmedia

While the Occupy Wall Street effort sincerely wishes that no physical harm ever come to anyone, our revolutionary nature also inspires us to tell these cronies of the 1-Percenters: "Come on, you guys. Trying being good Americans for once. Give us a clear voice, a chance to speak our minds without misinformation and without interruption."

Nonetheless, such demagoguery and ass-kissing of the Mega Wealthy is likely to continue these shady news analysis programs. After all, the small political minds of O'Reilly and Hannity might very well be motivated by their own monstrously huge personal assets.

Hannity reportedly earns tens of millions of dollars for his one-sided, un-American propaganda radio show aired by Clear Channel Communications. Added to these personal earnings, Hannity's TV income reportedly puts him within the certifiable class of 1-Percenters—all while trying to come off to his fans as "one of us."

O'Reilly occasionally hints on his show that he earns tens of millions of dollars as a TV commentator and best-selling author. Needless to say, as yet another small-minded conservative, as a 1-Percenter does he have a personal interest in portraying our vital revolution as meaningless, insignificant and barely worthy of mention?

Rather than become overly discouraged by the huge power within the hands of these wealthy few, those determined to press forward with this peaceful cause should keep in mind such enlightening statements by Hugo Black, the late U.S. Senator and United States Supreme Court justice: "The framers (of the constitution) knew that free speech is the friend of change and revolution. But they also knew that it is the deadliest enemy of tyranny."

Loudspeakers for the Rich Thrive

Many of us within the Occupy Movement realize that biased conservative media personalities such as O'Reilly and Hannity actually support the "tyranny of the 1-Percent"—the silent, unspoken acts of war by the Rich, inflicted upon the masses.

The chairman, CEO and founder of the News Corporation, billionaire Rupert Murdoch, shows in supporting or employing such wacko personalities that he embraces efforts by the Wealthy to "hate the poor."

Yes, while we embrace and encourage peace and a loving strategy, the O'Reillys, Hannitys and Murdochs of the world actively and aggressively show their hate and contempt for the poor and the former middle-class.

As these imbeciles press forward with their "let-them-eat-cake" attitudes, those of us Occupiers who seek positive, decisive and effective change yearn to focus on getting our urgent message out in a clear and concise manner.

Like Nathan Hale, we cherish liberty, while also fully cognizant that those who seek to shut down or to distort our message are not even close to being "great Americans."

During Hannity's radio program, he professes to know what such a person is—often anointing people with a fascist oriented with such a designation. Yet we fully realize that in the true sense of the word, a certifiable Great American is the kind of person who can stand tall, peacefully warding off his brand of hogwash.

CHAPTER 28
The Liberal Media Failed the USA

As if refusing to be outdone by their conservative counterparts in the competence category, those in the liberal media also fell flat on their faces in getting our message out.

Key among these incompetent journalists are the supposed superstars over at the liberal-minded CNBC-TV network. For the most part, Chris Matthews and Rachel Maddow strived to incorrectly and blatantly portray the Occupy Movement as ultra-liberal.

Right off the bat, such an inaccurate and insensitive label tells the general public that we're the kind of crazies that yearn for the government to give everyone a home at taxpayers' expense and cushy, high-paying government jobs.

As a Rhodes Scholar holding a PhD in philosophy, Maddow should know better than to paint the Occupy Movement into a proverbial corner. Too lazy to do her homework in the real world, she wants the public to swallow a bullshit line that portrays us as unaware and perhaps ignorant of the many difficulties in our political future.

Matthews appears out of touch with reality, looking and behaving as if 93 years old although only in his mid-60s. Matthews' on-air guffaws show his inability to grasp the intricate and often difficult-to-explain details of the vital Occupy Movement cause.

The Ultra-Liberal Keith Olbermann Sucks, Too

The over-the-top liberal commentary of Keith Olbermann, at Current TV babbles like a "Star Wars" jabberwocky on his "Countdown" show.

In early 2011, Olbermann parted ways with MSNBC after an apparent contract dispute. Could his anti-conservative leanings have ruffled too many feathers by criticizing Jeffrey R. Immelt, the fat cat at General Electric—the anti-American, anti-99-Percenter who moved that company's X-ray division jobs to China—after being appointed by President Obama to a task force organized creating U.S. employment?

Keep in mind here that General Electric owns 49 percent of NBC Universal, the parent company of the MSNBC operations plus various media-related outlets.

Yes, both the ultra-liberals and the neo-conservatives who dominate the news media have failed us miserably—especially when their positions are extreme on either side of the basic political spectrum.

And, the 51-percent owner of NBC Universal is Comcast, the world's largest cable TV operator which depends on greasy lobbyists and raunchy politicians to push through legislation designed to help ensure the continued viability and prosperity of its operations.

Indeed, the very 1-Percenters that we seek to legally neutralize via our revolution hold virtually all of the significant playing cards when dictating media commentary—both on the right and the left.

Insider Shenanigans Prevail

Born with a platinum spoon in his mouth, Comcast Chairman and CEO Brian L. Roberts is the son of the company's co-founder, Ralph J. Roberts.

Is the MSNBC and NBC Universal Conglomerate as shifty and conniving in pushing through their own self-serving liberal agenda as Murdoch has been at squeaking the Fox News Network's conservative agenda into the public mindset.

Whatever the answer, the perennial overall loser here remains the vast majority of the American public—robbed of essential, vital information by the various excessively political, highly biased media propaganda machines.

Both on the right and the left, these unprofessional journalists and shady news organizations essentially are thumbing their noses at our citizenry.

Ultimately, overall public opinion polls on Occupy-related issues hinge largely on what people see or hear through these various media. Sadly, those of us who yearn to get the accurate word out through the general news industry find only widespread misinformation there.

CHAPTER 29
Our Revolution Must Intensify

"Those who make peaceful revolution impossible make violent revolution inevitable," said John F. Kennedy, the 35th President of the United States.

Indeed, public officials who have hampered our Occupy Movement's peaceful attempts to gather across the U.S. and worldwide often increase our anger.

As the initial weeks, months and years after the birth of our movement click into full gear, elected leaders and regular folks worldwide are learning a key lesson about us.

Perhaps most of all, we shall never be stopped in our quest, even as our struggle pushes forward and our membership scrambles to define specific goals.

"I think that people want peace so much that one of these days governments had better get out of the way and let them have it," said Dwight David Eisenhower, 34th President of the United States and a five-star general in the U.S. Army.

As our movements swells and our communication systems

solidify, we seek to start out fast in efficiently solidifying into a peaceful army. Rather than getting shuffled aside as if meaningless whiners, we refuse to "shut up" and keep quiet about the most critical issues at this pivotal time in human history.

Without Us Society Would Deteriorate

If left unchecked and unencumbered, the world's largest corporations and 1-Percenters would eventually have most people worldwide living in abject poverty.

Meantime, there are many among us Occupy 99-Percenters who deeply love the United States, particularly our supposed freedoms of speech—although the overall media strives to keep us mum and under wraps.

All along, many within our ranks also know full well that "democracy sucks," except in a much different way than communism, socialism, fascism and dictatorships.

At face value, we're lead to believe that this republic gives people a "choice" because we have the supposed ability to vote for our elected leaders. Yet that system had once given the vast majority of Americans a false sense of security, when in fact all along the nation's corrupt politicians are all mere cronies controlled by powerbrokers.

"The surest way to corrupt a youth is to instruct him to hold in higher esteem those who think alike, than those who think differently," said Friedrich Nietzsche, a 19th Century German philosopher.

Sure enough, many of us within the Occupy Struggle have had to "think out of the box," in order to see and to target the actual problems that threaten societies worldwide. Any attempt on our part to do otherwise would fail to work in the best interests of a vast majority of the earth's population.

Let Us Act With Speed and Efficiency

"If I had eight hours to chop down a tree, I'd spend six hours sharpening the axe," said Abraham Lincoln, 16th President of the United States.

Embracing such a philosophy, while fully cognizant of the fact that our ideology sucks just like all other political ideologies, the Occupy Moment needs to realize and appreciate the need to work effectively and diligently to sharpen our plan, strategy and organization.

Along the way, we also must remain fully mindful that the violence inflected upon us and the strategies employed to silence our words are likely to increase as this revolution intensifies in scope and intensity.

"Great minds discuss ideas, average minds discuss events, and small minds discuss people," said Eleanor Roosevelt, wife and widow of Franklin Delano Roosevelt, 32nd President of the United States.

In a sense, all within a short period of time, in order to emerge as successful our quest must encapsulate and energize all three aspects of the human experience recognized by this late First Lady—ideas, events and people. Only through the gatherings of interested people at substantial public events can we catapult our honorable ideas into reality.

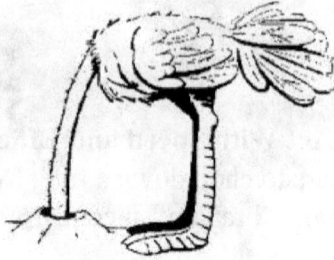

CHAPTER 30
Most People Prefer to Live in Denial

Terrified of the difficult coming changes and eager to live in the status quo, a huge majority of people today prefer to live in denial.

Politicians and top corporate leaders refuse to admit that virtually all government systems stink, particularly the current system under which we live.

Yes, not a single elected leader today has the gumption to stand tall and publicly state, "My political party stinks—all of them do, and we're all bought and paid for."

Sadly, until such time as such puppets start acting reasonably and level-headed, the disparity between the extremely rich and the very poor will continue to widen.

"The accomplice to the crime of corruption is frequently our own indifference," said Bess Myerson, a former Miss America who has been involved in New York politics.

All Our Strategies and Leadership Gets Lambasted

Adding to our organization's early birth pangs, some analysts view the initial Occupy leadership from a "damned-if-we-do," and "damned-if-we-don't" perspective.

On a local, state, national and worldwide basis, some of our various leaders and organizers have strived to hide behind anonymity—preferring to state that this "is a people's organization. It's not about its leaders." When this happens, we're characterized as weak, insignificant socialists without any backbone.

And, when some members have sought to take a strong, vibrant public role in stating reasons and strategies, they're soundly booed for being too dictatorial or for failing to let the vast numbers of people among our ranks control our destiny.

When viewed from an indifferent, non-biased perspective, all these challenges might seem to indicate that the Occupy Movement is in a "lose-lose" situation.

To the contrary, however, our collective journey has taken a positive route by finally beginning to blossom worldwide—something that probably should have clicked into full gear several decades ago.

Our Necessary Chore ~ Focus

"Corruption and hypocrisy ought not be inevitable products of democracy as they are today," said Mahatma Gandhi, the India philosopher and peace activist assassinated in 1948 at age 78.

For many of us, democracy reigns as by far the most viable and ideal of all the many evil governmental systems. At least through such processes the people hold certain rights supposedly designed to give them power to enact positive change.

Herein rests the core challenge for our Occupy Soldiers, the short- and long-term abilities to identify and target specific problems while effectively implementing solutions. Until such time as we have a clear, focused and stated mission, our quest shall meander like a rudderless ship on the ocean, without even a captain or a crew.

An age-old saying tells us that "every man has his price." When embracing this way of thinking, we're supposed to think that all societies worldwide will always eventually cave in to corruption—particularly within democracies.

U.S. Sen. John Kerry, a Massachusetts Democrat who campaigned as his party's nominee in the 2004 presidential election, has been quoted as saying: "It's a sad day when you have members of Congress who are literally criminals go undisciplined by their colleagues. No wonder people look at Washington and know this city is broken."

Angry

CHAPTER 31
Our Anger Intensified

The individual and collective anger of Occupy Warriors surged, thanks largely to social media systems that enabled us to share the atrocities inflicted upon us by 1-Percenters.

The selfish behaviors of politicians sparked just as much ire as the wonton, reckless actions of huge corporations that literally put the public in physical danger.

But lots of us know that effective results and a clear plan can only emerge if we keep our growing displeasure at bay. By showing only anger and frustration, we would essentially become weak—increasingly vulnerable to attack and disruption.

During the autumn of 2011 as our quest began its initial, sudden and significant growth, news leaked that huge corporations continued their pattern of proverbially slapping the little guy in the face.

Key examples sprang into the public consciousness when— pushed to the point of frustration—numerous health organizations stepped up efforts to get the Johnson & Johnson company to stop using potentially cancer-causing substances in its baby shampoo. Giving an answer that failed to satisfy some organizations, the company then announced that it has been working since 2009 to phase out the substances.

Such a devil-may-care attitude leapfrogged into numerous other corporations, including the JetBlue commercial airline. Reckless and shameless, indifferent to the suffering of many people, the airline let passengers wait in one of its jets for seven full hours while parked on a runway during a snowstorm in Hartford, Connecticut. Toilets overflowed as anger peaked, before the airline later issued a meaningless public apology.

Corporate America Flips the Finger to Consumers

The Johnson & Johnson case and the JetBlue incident are just two of the many hundreds or thousands of instances where Corporate America literally tramples over the rights and safety concerns of all consumers.

With politicians in their back pockets, huge corporations keep testing the limits of compromising public safety.

Echoing their party lines, particularly conservatives, these cronies proclaim that "trial attorneys" are scumbags for daring to sue Corporate America for endangering the public.

Under this line of thinking, we're supposed to believe that any jury awards should be limited to just a few thousand dollars—while consumers should put all their faith and trust in Big Companies and in Congress, neither which gives a poop about people.

Latching onto the longtime public mindset that puts attorneys in bed with devils, these fruitcakes—especially those on the conservative or Republican side—complain that corporations pay far too much in legal fees—ultimately resulting in higher prices for consumers.

Should We Kill All the Lawyers?

"The first thing we do, let's kill all the lawyers," said William Shakespeare, the legendary British bard from the late 16th and early 17th Centuries.

On a serious note, our culture dives into the darkest realms of an evil mentality when we allow Big Corporations to operate unchecked without giving lawyers at least some opportunity to take huge bites out of the greedy ass of American Industry.

"We all know that the law is the most powerful of schools for the imagination," said Jean Giraudoux, a French novelist, essayist and playwright in the early 20th Century.

Too much power on either side, either in favor of consumers or in the corner of Big Companies, could very well cripple either the economy or public health.

Unless we all collectively reach a reasonable balance on both fronts, if the current trend continues Big Corporations will continue to destroy the world's environment with ever-increasing frequency.

CHAPTER 32
Avoid Demonizing Capitalism

Shamefully using scare tactics, many political cronies strive to convince the public that the Occupy Soldiers are striving to "demonize capitalism."

From the view of these ill-informed prognosticators, most of them in the pocket of 1-Percenters, those of us in the 99-Percent supposedly think that earning big money is evil.

To the contrary, however, whatever the Rich might want you to believe, a vast majority of us within the Occupy Movement know that efforts to lawfully earn money can be a healthy part of the process—at least when certain counterbalances are in place.

A healthy, vibrant business-friendly economic environment unfettered by over-burdensome taxes and needless regulations can and should generate plenty of good-paying jobs.

Sadly, though, significant major problems can occur when the balance between workers and fat-cats gets far out of whack. By some estimates, today's CEOs, top executives and board chairmen sometimes earn many hundreds or even tens of thousands times more than their front-line personnel.

Economic surveys have indicated that this diverse trend has worsened in recent decades. The spending-power of the little person keeps dwindling, while the buying strength of the corporate elite reaches levels that would make monarchs envious.

They Portray us as Robin Hood

Our many detractors also strive to make the public believe that as an overall group, the Occupy Movement wants to essentially emerge as a so-called modern Robin Hood.

Under this warped line of thinking, we're supposedly seeking to rip off at least 20 percent of the assets of the Wealthy—before handing over these funds directly to the poor, even uneducated individuals or people who flat-out refuse to work.

This propaganda is designed to enrage the general public against us, for supposedly having a plan to give every person a high salary and a good house even in instances where individuals refuse to get a good education or to engage in employment.

Obviously, such a "free-ticket-for-the-poor" system would wreck and perhaps permanently destroy any hopes for a good, solid economy. All workers and even entrepreneurs would lose their incentive to work and to produce, resulting in a faltering economic system mired in muck.

Forced into a position of responsibility, many of us within the Occupy Movement recognize, appreciate and respect the need for balance in all matters involving money.

Our Enemies Behave Like Numbskulls

Continually on the offensive, our detractors also seek to paint devilish horns on our heads. These pirates of ineptitude, particularly ultra conservatives, portray us as an overall group as drugged-out thieves, rapists and double-talkers who don't give a shit about the environment.

Numerous high-paid media pundits cite infrequent incidents of narcotics abuse at Occupy rallies, a solitary report of sexual harassment at one such function and trash left behind at a handful of these events as signaling that Occupy Warriors don't give a hoot about anyone other than themselves.

Since the primary objective of any propaganda campaign is to demonize the opponent, these media goons seek to portray our average revolutionary as "young, stoned, horny people prone to thievery, and who want a free ride for the rest of their lives."

While this undoubtedly must be the case among a handful participants at our rallies, our overall membership seems to contain a diverse segment of the overall population that yearns to find or to create good-paying employment.

When all is said and done, for the most part we know and fully appreciate the fact that the vast majority of Occupy Soldiers are good, decent, kind and God-loving people who love the potential that America can provide.

CHAPTER 33
War Looms on the Horizon

Weather our many Occupy Soldiers like to admit this or not, the many enemies of the United States threaten our nation with actual, all-out physical war.

Besides terrorists from the Middle East, the corrupt nations of Russia and China have been actively building their militaries in recent years, according to news accounts.

War involving wide-scale murder sucks even more than starvation, corrupt governments and ineffective political philosophy.

While Occupy Wall Street activists love the freedom to generate effective change, we abhor and avoid any and all type of physical violence. All along, we realize that amid these extremely stressful times poop-heads from around the globe are eager to attack us.

Added to this mix, we must also consider the violent-oriented U.S. citizens.

If the charges are true, militiamen who allegedly planned an attack on U.S. government facilities in the Atlanta area in the fall of 2011 have shit for brains. Other fuck-ups include the creeps in the Al-Qaeda terrorist network that attacked America in 2001, killing thousands and launching wars that took the lives of many U.S. citizens.

Warriors Want to Destroy the USA

The fuckers among the Taliban operating in Afghanistan deserve plenty of our contempt as well, especially when they slaughter people and treat women like pigs.

Throughout numerous nations across Africa pea-brained warlords steal food from starving families, leaving children to die while slaying adults with bullets and machetes.

Wickedness permeates every corner of the globe.

Even though we would like to believe that a vast majority of people are kind and eager to help others without causing anyone harm, history keeps repeating itself even today—marked by murder and greed.

"You cannot simultaneously prevent and prepare for war," said Albert Einstein, the iconic genius of the 19th and 20th Centuries.

A reliable fact-check and analysis of the current dangers shows unequivocally that without a strong military and a reliable intelligence program, the United States can and will fall to those who yearn to see us suffer.

Without Soldiers for Protection We Will Die

Many of us within the Occupy Movement, particularly those better than 60 years old, like to romanticize the anti-war efforts of

95

the late 1960s and early 1970s. The so-called Hippy Generation was right on track in making their opinions clear, that war sucks.

While such sentiments might seem more admirable than ever today, however, the cold and difficult facts tell us that having a strong, vibrant and effective military is among the "evil necessities" of life.

Thus, even though many Occupy Soldiers would like to dismantle the U.S. military, the wisest thinkers among our ranks realize that any attempt to severely slash the United States defense budget would be a serious and fatal mistake.

"I know not with what weapons World War III will be fought, but World War IV will be fought with sticks and stones," Einstein said.

While the cost of supporting and maintaining a military might be deemed too excessive, the potential consequences of failing to keep such a force are far more severe than anyone could possibly comprehend.

CHAPTER 34
Critical Thinking Becomes Essential

The extreme challenges facing our world today leaves our educated Occupy Warriors saddled with the urgent, necessary need to engage in critical thinking.

At no time until now in all of human history has the human race faced this type of a widespread dilemma on such a critical scale. Today's instant digital technology, complex interwoven financial systems and difficult challenges make our quest formidable.

Perhaps more than ever before, differing value and moral systems generate and intensify growing conflict between the Wealthy Elite and the Lower Economic Class.

In essence, everything comes down to a handful of human-based systems that people have studied, created and tweaked for thousands of years.

The answers and solutions shall remain a matter of intense debate, until such time as people can generate an accurate, irrefutable gauge or barometer that effectively monitors results on a monetary and life-quality scale.

Consider These Unique and Vital Factors

Amid the increasingly intense conflict between the Wealthy 1-Percenters and the downtrodden financially strapped 99-Percenters everything hinges on these major factors:

Philosophy: Differing and converging thoughts on the morality and the use of various strategies—including whether to "level the playing field" among adversaries. For instance, should combatants remain peaceful or resort to violence? And, what is considered "moral" to one group or individual might be considered "highly immoral" to another.

Economics: In today's highly complex financial world pulverized by complex systems ranging from derivatives to futures, which formulas should be used—and who should benefit the most?

Should the poor be excluded from this "game," or should more be done to lessen the seemingly unbreakable power of the rich—their rules and minimum-trading requirements now preventing the poor from big-gain potential.

Psychology: What is the mental breaking point of the poor and of the rich? When and how is each motivated to acquiesce or compromise to the others' needs, or motivated to ignore or balk at the demands of their counterparts?

Spirituality: How if at all does a person or a society's spiritual or religious beliefs come to play? How and when, if at all, should a segment of the population be forced to follow such dogma? And, just as important, how might a person reject such edicts?

Our Strategies Became Strong and True

Throughout the ages, humans have written countless volumes and pontificated about the differing strategies and morals that involve philosophy, economics, psychology and spirituality.

For our part, many of us within the Occupy Movement embrace a philosophy that demands or at least encourages strength, fortitude and love within our membership. When everything is said and done, we adore and cherish each human being and want the best for every person.

Yet our philosophy also gives a right, in fact a requirement, to protect ourselves especially when someone is shooting at us or robbing us or preventing us from earning what we deserve.

On the economics front, we encourage and seek a world where each person is required and encouraged to have "personal responsibility" for his or her pathway in life—especially if, and only if, such a route is on a "level and fair" playing field.

Within the realm of psychology, this does not mean by any stretch of the imagination that every person in the world should have "equal" finances. Doing so would destroy the need for diverse classes of people—the essential need for motivation to work.

Ultimately, on the spiritual level, we soundly reject any belief or spiritual dogma that forces or mandates specific behaviors or enacts restrictions on the masses. When and if such lunacy emerges, we must and shall fight to soundly overthrow such temporary hierarchy.

CHAPTER 35
Beware of the New World Order

While some people insist such worries are over-the-top paranoia, many of our Occupy Warriors realize that the Wealthy or perhaps even liberals might be striving to create a "New World Order."

Under this theory or objective, all primary governments would conspire to create an international authoritarian system operated by the Wealthy or by flaky "progressives."

Anyone serious about serving as an effective Occupy Soldier needs to know and acknowledge this fact. Quietly and behind the scenes, for many years the super-elite likely have been working to create the basic foundations for such a system.

The process encompasses all-consuming propaganda, disseminating information that misleads the public. Today's so-called mainstream news media seems to have already perpetuated and embraced this stereotype.

Analysts and sociologists argue about the reliability of such claims. Yet many of us within the Occupy Movement have consistently seen clear and undeniable signs that such a transition is in place, especially on the economic front.

Conspiracy Theorists Go Bananas

Some conspiracy theorists claim that two primary realms within U.S. Society are responsible for generating such a system.

Many of us worry that fanatic fundamentalist Christians and anti-government fanatics on the far right have either pushed for or vehemently opposed authoritarian rule on a national and international basis.

According to numerous online reports, since Obama's initial inauguration in January 2009, his administration has played a crucial role in pushing for a one-world government.

In April of that year, on his conservative Fox News Network show Bill O'Reilly said that some people "believe Speaker Nancy Pelosi [D-CA], Senator Harry Reid [D-NV], and President Obama himself are sympathetic to the one-world, global-justice view."

O'Reilly went on to say that a one-world government would "seize private property and distribute it so that every human being has roughly the same amount of resources."

Taking this a step further, on his nationally syndicated

conservative radio show at the time, Glenn Beck stated: "The Constitution is being taken apart piece by piece through international coalitions, through international law, and through the United Nations."

Any New World Order Would Stink

While no evidence of such a secretive effort by Obama and other governments exist, many within our Occupy ranks might hold justifiable worries about possible attempts to establish a New World Order.

Perhaps such statements by conservative commentators was used a smoke screen, an effort to scare liberals and particularly non-partisan, middle-of-the-road voters away from Obama's 2012 re-election campaigns.

Or, even more disturbing, perhaps discussions of creating such a system have occurred among world leaders—if only "on the hush," on a casual, informal basis.

Heaped in dogma and sucking in every possible conspiracy theory, do fundamentalist Christians view Obama as an anti-Christ? Do such individuals truly believe that liberals yearn to create a single global umbrella government?

To some of us within the Occupy Movement who consider ourselves as "thinkers" or at least critical analysts, the notion of a New World Order rings loud as frightening and highly disturbing. The notion of a single, unified world government controlling finances rattles us to the bone, especially a system that would enable a singular financial empire to fall under control of a single political ideology—either liberal or conservative.

CHAPTER 36
Danger Erupts From Insurgency

Danger intensifies, an increasing probability that a despotic, dictatorial public figure will emerge from the chaos if anarchy erupts as a result of worldwide discontent against the 1-Percenters.

Another lesson learned from throughout human history tells us that evil dictators emerge whenever the public seeks a leader who tells them what they want to hear.

Such opportunists seize the ideal chance to catapult to power when a society is weak, especially following wars and serious economic disruptions.

Those who assumed such roles during the past 150 years, slaughtering millions of people, included Joseph Stalin, Adolph Hitler, Idi Amin Dada, Mao Zedong, Pol Pot, Richard Nixon, and Benito Mussolini.

Many among our ranks of Occupy Warriors fear that anarchy will ensue if our movement erupts into violence, clearing the way for a dictatorial leader who will fool the masses—generating propaganda while slaughtering poor people every second.

Charismatic People Kill Millions

Such demons usually rise to the peak of power if and when the overall public becomes gullible enough to swallow a bunch of rhetorical bullshit.

Charismatic leaders such as James Warren "Jim" Jones, who generated the mass suicide of 909 Peoples Temple followers, tell the masses what they want to hear.

Statements such as: "We are better than other people," or "My system guarantees a way out of your economic plight," motivate many individuals to join the ranks the ranks of such charismatic creeps.

The followers usually are either: uneducated morons for the most part; people who fail to put much thought into joining sleazy political organizations; or those who sign up purely out of fear.

At all times, Occupy Warriors need to refrain and ward off any such efforts, especially because dictatorial systems suck far more than democracy. Everybody loses under dictatorships and extreme governmental systems, which always fall—usually in extensively bloody uprisings.

Never Trust Organization Leaders

Everyone involved in the Occupy Movement should be wary and revolt against any of our members who encourage extreme violence or push the words of a single leader.

The world is loaded with mega-talented, highly charismatic and corrupt people who possess compelling public speaking abilities. Such jerks push hot air through their mouths, babbling about supposed "hope" and "change" without delivering the goods.

The age-old saying that "might makes right" fails to carry weight here, largely because Occupy Warriors will never tolerate such hogwash.

Yet warding off such efforts to control us might become increasingly difficult, particularly if and when the Wealthy 1-Percenters or any new regime uses the latest digital technology to make any attempts at a peaceful revolt almost impossible.

Various news reports indicate that the corrupt U.S. Congress is considering legislation enabling Internet hosting providers to spy on and shut down Web sites. Could this be a first step in censoring those who would dare to protest or to seek change in our corrupt government?

Worsening matters, additional technology is already well underway that would enable governments to put digital chips in our bodies—enabling authorities to track our every move from the hour of our births until eventual death.

Whether we like to admit this or not, the freedoms that we cherish and hold dear might very well disappear unless our movement remains continuously vigilant.

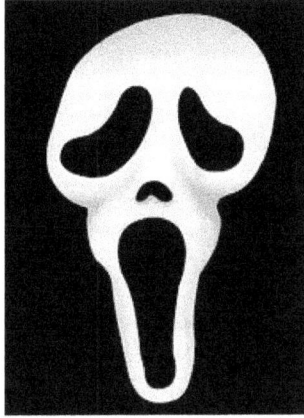

CHAPTER 37
Avoid Vigilante Justice

Cognizant of the ever-present need to reach our primary goals, all Occupy Soldiers also should avoid any urges to resort to mindless, fruitless vigilante justice.

Such actions would seek to either inflict physical harm or at least to imprison the Wealthy powerbrokers, stealing their possessions and eliminating them from society.

By engaging in such actions, we would become no better than our adversaries—definitely much worse them on a short-term and long-term basis.

Adding fuel to the flames, sudden devastating and injurious violence could very well disrupt or irreparably harm the basic infrastructure of society. As a result, we essentially would be "fighting against ourselves," damaging or hindering the possibility of re-establishing the vibrancy of the American middle class.

The writer and poet William Butler Yeats summed this up when stating: "Things fall apart, the center cannot hold. Mere anarchy is loosened upon the world. The blood-dimmed tide is loosened, and everywhere the ceremony of innocence is drowned. The best lack all conviction, while the worst are full of compassionate intensity."

Acting like mindless, stupid hotheads and inflicting violence also would force us to lose the hearts and alliance of the general public—anyone who has not actively joined our so-called peaceful war against the elite.

Already in some instances, our struggle to congregate in public places has forced some businesses to temporarily or even permanently close. This has forced numerous satellite stores and privately owned restaurants to close, resulting in layoffs.

So, amid our overall struggle to help the working class, due to short-sightedness by our leaders or the ignorance of our warriors, we have in some instances actually disrupted the lives and incomes of regular working people.

When this happens "we suck" just as much as those whom we complain about. Rather than hampering or severely damaging the already-fragile economy, we need to push forward hard and relentless in efforts to push through sensible, long-lasting change through effective legislation.

Thus, any anarchy on our part should remain peaceful and yet insurmountably powerful, strong and resilient in the face of widespread corruption throughout society.

Louis D. Brandeis, a U.S. Supreme Court justice in the early 1900s, publicly admitted that anarchy is inevitable at least in some form when the government becomes corrupt: "Our government teaches the whole people by its example. If the government becomes the lawbreaker, it breeds contempt for law; it invites every man to become a law unto himself; it invites anarchy."

CHAPTER 38
Corruption Permeates World
Financial Markets

Our most ardent warriors also need to realize the banking industries and the financial markets are loaded with corruption on a worldwide scale.

This evil-based system spans a vast range of cultures and governmental systems, from communist countries to democracies and even pseudo-socialism.

A key example of this devilish system hinges within the securities trading systems of the U.S. stock exchanges. The mega-wealthy control and hold exclusive rights to lightning fast super computers that automatically perform trades 24 hours a day.

These computers dictate which trades to make and when, making those decisions based on complex mathematical algorithms without people even being involved.

This scum-sucking, secretive system pushes the little guy at the proverbial bottom of the toilet, making the poor or disadvantaged non-elite unable to execute the best, most lucrative securities market trades on a consistent regular basis.

In fact, according to various news reports, all that the Super Rich benefiting from these auto-trading systems need to do is sit back and relax. All this happens around-the-clock, as continuous big money keeps rolling into the waiting arms of the Wealthy without them ever having to do a thing.

Wealth Has its Undeniable Advantages

Only an intense, decades-long effort by Occupy Warriors will be able to topple such entrenched injustices within the Wealthy's infrastructure.

Worsening matters, because only Rich people sit on boards of the largest corporations that control the world's logistics, these individuals are unlikely to relinquish their power or to give the poor an ability to make a decent living on a consistent basis.

As if all this weren't already enough to make the little guy sick to his stomach, the Wealthy or highly funded social organizations can legally amass Political Action Committees or PACs. These funds can and do support the puppet politicians, enabling them to crush their opponents via devious governmental legislation.

Yes, money is perhaps the most powerful weapon of all in this urgent battle between the rich and the poor.

Although some within the Occupy leadership initially collected hundreds of thousands of dollars for our cause, that pales by comparison to the billions of dollars that the Rich can and will use in an attempt to literally crush our cause.

We Can and Should Amass Substantial Funds

With all this in mind, let us forget about the age-old adage even though it might be true, that: "Money is the root of all evil."

On the flip side of this coin, as we press forward in our battle those of us Occupiers who fight this revolution in a thoughtful manner know that we can and will amass our own legally authorized "super-funds." When $1 bills and $5 bills get collected consistently in massive numbers, the total can approach billions—even in a one-year period.

Yet the general public on a widespread, grassroots scale is unlikely to donate those amounts if they perceive us as a bunch of violent fruitcakes burning down homes, blocking businesses and causing needless violence in the streets.

Yes, money can and will play a key, essential role in doing us—the poor—a world of good in positively and effectively pushing forward with this valiant, necessary quest.

Plato, the ancient Greek philosopher summed this up, proclaiming: "Those who are too smart to engage in politics are punished by being governed by those who are dumber." Embracing this philosophy, Occupiers who once avoided politics now find themselves yearning to participate in a positive way.

CHAPTER 39
Legitimate Jobs Remain Available

Mired in understandable frustration, many of the unemployed even within the Occupy ranks have given up all hope of every finding legitimate job online.

Yet for those crafty enough to believe good, solid work still exists, numerous work positions still can be found—particularly for online-based employment.

The key here is to remember that some systems operate as scams, ripping off desperate consumers who hope to generate income from their homes.

Eager to help the unemployed land some income, some Occupy Advocates experienced at such job-hunt efforts urge stress the need for money-back guarantees.

If a company or potential employer fails to offer to return your funds on a no-questions-asked basis within 60 days, avoid them at all costs and tell such programs to "go fly a kite." Based on what we've heard through extensive research, one of the best such opportunities can be found at http://www.BushLite.com

While legitimate and lucrative employment remains extremely difficult to find in many regions, Occupy Participants with extensive connections in the job world have an obligation to give suggestions to our unemployed soldiers.

To accomplish, one of the most successful Internet entrepreneurs in the USA has launched a training program, where he offers participants a 60-day money back guarantee for those seeking to learn how to make a living online. Those details can be found at http://www.SuperPowerline.com

While lots of our members continue a desperate hunt for jobs that seem almost nowhere to be found, many of Occupy Warriors have simply given up hope.

Who could blame our jobless comrades for feeling discouraged, especially after the 1-Percenters essentially "rigged the system" by betting that many mortgage holders would fail to pay off their debts?

Francis Ann "Fran" Lebowitz, an American writer and humorist, has been quoted as saying that "In the Soviet Union, capitalism triumphed over communism. In this country, capitalism triumphed over democracy."

Amazingly, creative Occupy Movement activists can employ various digital methods to earn themselves money—all while using, producing and distributing YouTube videos featuring our various protests.

To accomplish this, Occupy Soldiers can sign up for accounts by visiting http://www.EmergencyHandbooks.com

The system enables users to use Facebook and other social media platforms to spread their videos virally worldwide, while generating income for them in the process—potentially spreading their messages virally across the Internet.

A wide variety of other income-for-networking programs are available.

This seems logical and even necessary. After all, every major and significant revolution in world history has been forced to devise creative and workable methods of generating massive funds—for their individual members and their overall programs.

Without any question whatsoever, devising creative and legal methods of earning money becomes admirable and even necessary for many of us to remain fully engaged in this vital revolution.

CHAPTER 40
Wicked Governments Imitate Insects

Contributing to the public's growing anger against the federal government, politicians and bureaucracies have funneled monies to incompetent private companies.

Many of these businesses have been run by Wealthy significant contributors to major political campaigns of the politicians who work these backroom deals.

A prime example that sparked the public's ire became Solyndra, a California solar cell panel company that received a $535 million loan from the U.S. Department of Energy.

This sappy taxpayer-funded deal came as the news media revealed that a major Obama campaign fund contributor, Oklahoma billionaire George Kaiser, had been linked to a venture capital fund—among Solyndra's biggest investors.

The stench of slimy politics led some Republicans to wonder whether the funding deal had been rushed through in an effort to assist significant campaign contributors.

This case marks just one of perhaps hundreds—if not thousands—of backroom, pork-barrel government deals that benefited corporations owned by the Wealthy.

Government's Failures Create a Domino Effect

Besides the problems of complex international and domestic financial systems set in place to benefit 1-Percenters, Occupiers also face the gargantuan task of obliterating slime in government.

Various political puppets engage in behind-the-scenes trickery, while also striving to cut back on vital public disclosure laws.

Thumbing their nose at the public, as our movement grew in depth and scope, several members of Congress proposed weakening the federal Freedom of Information Act. Under the proposal submitted on the sly by these political goons, federal officials would essentially be allowed to pick and choose which Freedom of Information Act applications they would like to answer. At present, journalists and interested citizens use the act's application process to investigate our government's activities.

This marks a sharp contrast to current regulations, which for the most part make almost all federal documents a matter of public record. The only current exceptions involve cases such as the protection of certain personal privacy data such as income tax documents, or matters deemed secret for reasons involving national security.

"The secret of life is honesty and fair dealing. If you can fake that, you've got it made," said Groucho Marx, a 20th Century movie and stage comic.

The U.S. Government Could Give a Shit About Freedom

Raising the ire of Occupy Supporters worldwide, governments

113

and corporations have become increasingly secretive in recent years—particularly in so-called democracies such as the United States where the people supposedly benefit from "freedom of speech."

Yet one of the best ways for government and politicians to avoid criticism is to work out of the public limelight, while keeping virtually everything essential secret—under the supposed guise of supposed national security.

All along, the actual and ultimate purpose of such shenanigans is to protect the Wealthy, push forward the wicked agenda of 1-Percenters, and essentially squish mud smack-dab into the faces of all us supposed "little guys."

"It has been said that democracy is the worst form of government, except all the others that have been tried," said Winston Churchill, prime minister of Great Britain during World War II.

While many Occupy supporters might embrace Churchill's sentiments, we also must recognize the need to keep government skullduggery under tight scrutiny.

CHAPTER 41
Europe Faces Another Difficult Challenge

Intensifying our efforts on an international scale, Europe faces its own unique and formidable Occupy Movement challenges.

Numerous governments across that continent are saddled with burdensome debt that likely will cause severe worldwide economic upheaval.

Much of the blame for this critically harmful debt stems from efforts by various governments such as those in Greece, Italy, Spain and England to create huge government-operated "nanny states."

While corporations across Europe remained typically selfish and evil for the most part, workers in numerous societies and diverse countries sought and demanded cushy, lucrative retirements in exchange for doing relatively little work.

Heightening the problem even more, many workers and labor organizations rammed through lucrative government-sponsored pension programs that were to become effective at extremely low retirement ages—in some instances as low as 55 or even the relatively young age of just 50.

Doomsday Faces the Entire World

While this might sound like a "doomsday" prediction, collective and seemingly insurmountable debt within the Euro-zone is likely to ultimately cause an extensive, severe and catastrophic worldwide economic collapse.

The biggest crisis that Europe has faced since World War II will click into gear from 2012 through 2013 and far beyond, an extreme financial crisis causing extreme poverty.

While rioting, rampant murders and chaos race across Europe and spread deep into Asia, the entire region will lack a clear, definable leader—until such time as one might emerge.

This so-called domino effect will ravage international financial markets, sending all economies into an endless, inescapable whirlpool.

For all this, we will be able to thank the 1-Percenters of

115

the world, plus many of the people throughout Europe who demanded socialistic or communist-like forms of government.

Expect Starvation to Spread Worldwide

Partly as a result, even without having the Occupy Movement as an impetus, rioting and civil wars will erupt around the globe.

Hand-to-hand combat will blanket almost every major city ept;feofr, as people fight each other for basic necessities such as food.

Although the primary communications systems such as the generally corrupt news media should remain in place, the international logistical system designed to produce and transport goods will deteriorate.

Throughout the United States, many of the things we take for granted such as the purchase of electronic devices like cell phones—which usually only last two or three years per unit—will whither.

Meantime, as virtually all major currencies collapse including the U.S. dollar, many U.S. residents will learn sadly and far too late that their nation has become far too dependent on food grown in other countries.

With supermarket shelves across America empty or nearly bare, rare commodities such as gold and silver will skyrocket in price. But merely having precious metals will do little if anything to ensure survival. A person can have all the gold in the world but if there is no food to purchase, then that individual starves.

CHAPTER 42
Acknowledge the Doomsday Scenario

As many of us learned form childhood, the tale of Chicken Little—also known as "Chicken Licken" or "Henny Penny"—involved a character who mistakenly believes the end of the world is imminent, only to eventually discover otherwise.

Throughout history, many people have been roundly accused of being "Chicken Littles," but some of them were subsequently proven right on the mark when extreme tragedies occurred at least in a short-term regional sense.

During the final years before the launch of the American Civil War, numerous people predicted a bloody confrontation. Among them was abolitionist John Brown, hanged for treason against the Union Army a few years before the war erupted.

The ultimate outbreak of World War II across Europe and the Asia-Pacific region came as no surprise to many longtime political observers.

Of course, throughout history there also have been plenty of certified Chicken Littles in human form, primarily fruitcakes who predicted incorrectly that the world would suddenly come to an end due to over-the-top religious dogma.

Precious Metals Prices Skyrocket

Behind the scenes, some business leaders and advocates of buying precious metals have predicted many of the current struggles for several years.

As virtually all world currencies lose their value, certain rare tangible, tradable and transferable assets such as gold have soared upward in price.

Through the first decade of the 21st Century, some analysts writing at the KitCo precious metals Website have predicted rioting in the streets, the collapse of financial markets, and even "class warfare."

Lots of us within the Occupy Movement have hoped and prayed that many who marched beside us would refrain from unnecessary violence—but that has been far from the case. Even when shuttling such concerns aside, there can be no denying what all of us with TVs, radios and the Internet see increasingly on a daily basis.

Violence and chaos are spreading rapid-fire around the globe, at a far more rapid, wide-scale rate than ever before. From its inception in late September 2011, the Occupy Wall Street movement raced to hundreds of cities nationwide and around the globe.

The Huge, Wide-Scale Movement Became Unstoppable

By the end of 2011, the rage, scope and intensity of the

Occupy Movement swelled and grew so much on a national and worldwide scale that all-out chaos became imminent.

In summary, our movement has become unstoppable.

Whether some of us want this to happen or not, especially while lacking clear and strong leadership, our quest is likely to last for many years to come.

In defiance of the peaceful among our ranks, as many of us fear and fully expect—although we never want that to happen— many over-the-top revolutionaries likely will resort to fruitless and unnecessary violence.

These projections worsen even more when taking into account that overall the Occupy Wall Street movement lacks clearly stated, succinct and definable goals other than obliterating the disparity between the Super Rich and the poor.

CHAPTER 43
Pray for Peace Despite the Odds

Unable to curtail the violent efforts of the few extreme communist or socialist fanatics who incorrectly claim to be among our accepted ranks, those of us who stress the need for ongoing love and peace are likely to shed many tears in the months and years to come.

As far as many of us know, there is no one, single highly respected person who can definitely announce to the world and get a positive answer: "Violent revolutionaries, those of you among the Occupy Movement around the world, put down your arms. Behave in a common-sense fashion and work toward your goals in a peaceful way."

Unless a sudden hero emerges—a wide, charismatic and level-headed person championing the rights of 1-Percenters—lots of us fear that the snot-nosed jerks among us who insist upon violence will wreak non-stop havoc upon the world.

Violence would only worsen problems, creating far more difficulties than the extreme hardships that we already face.

Avoid Causing Direct Physical Harm

With this challenge clearly understood, fully cognizant of the urgent need to refrain from violence, those among our ranks with common sense need to seize the baton representing peace.

Now is the time to push long and hard for a non-violent solution, careful to avoid causing direct physical harm to anyone.

While lacking a distinct, widely respected leader or figurehead, we need to show that positive results can and will come about as long as we remain peaceful and vigilant. To do otherwise would be to fail ourselves, our families, our friends and people everywhere.

Every step of the way, we should fully acknowledge that our Occupy Movement sucks, that our quest should not be considered the "be-all, and end-all solution."

When and if our comrades are murdered by police or the military, and some of us fear that likely will happen, we should continue to insist on peace. Fighting with fire on our part will only serve to get a similar but far more massive response aimed in our direction—total conflagration and near annihilation.

They Want to Shoot us Dead

Championing our urgent cause, let us also realize that many graves likely will be filled with the bodies of our comrades.

Around the world, particularly in Syria, Egypt, Yemen and elsewhere in the Middle East, the ultra-Rich 1-Percenters have been all too happy to shoot us down.

Among the worst possible scenarios would be for all-out civil war to erupt across the United States. While continually pressing forward with our Occupy gatherings and protests in many cities, we should at all times strive to refrain from military-style attacks, concentrating instead on widespread civil unrest.

Like the peace-armies of obedient, non-violent protestors led by Gandhi and Martin Luther King, we need to press forward in relentless, non-stop action in such a loving manner.

Only through peace can we show strength, get positive results and ultimately change the world for the better.

CHAPTER 44
Keep Moving Toward Our Primary Goals

All Occupy advocates need to continually keep moving toward our primary objectives, although our organization keeps developing its official stated goals.

The primary objective remains to level the playing field between the Rich and the 99-Percenters—giving us equal power in the political process.

When that occurs, key strides will occur when Occupiers generate fail-safe systems designed to lessen and eliminate corruption in government and in the corporate world.

Acknowledging that no "utopian society" will ever emerge as possible, we also need to give people motivation to work and to become productive. This way, each person can truly get positioned to earn the money that he or she deserves.

All along, we need to limit the size of government, because otherwise none of us will truly prosper. At its peak performance, the new improved system will not guarantee that all people are economically equal, but rather that working people earn a decent income while everyone gets a "fair shake."

Under the best and most efficient system, entrepreneurs, corporate executives and everyday people will be encouraged to learn as much as they can. Efficient, goal-oriented work also means adequate time for leisure and for much-needed rest and rejuvenation.

The Rule of Law is a Fraud

A key part of this process entails dismantling our so-called "rule of law," rebuilding regulations and oversight from bottom to top.

Before this essential stride can begin to happen, Occupiers need to play a significant role in dismantling and rebuilding campaign contribution laws. Ideally, all campaign contributions of any kind would become illegal, a step that would greatly piss off the 1-Percenters, lobbyists and crooked politicians that represent special interests.

Secondly, far short of declaring marshal law, we need to enact legislation that makes the formal lobbying process as we now know it the equivalent to felonious treason against the government of the United States.

At present, registered lobbyists have hundreds of times more political power than average citizens—who possess no significant voice whatsoever in the political process. Thus, in the reformed legislation, those in the lobbying industry and regular citizens would finally find themselves on an equal playing field with average citizens.

Under the revised legislation, "lobbying" in its now-traditional sense will become tantamount to jury tampering—except in this case such individuals would be engaging in "politician tampering." Within the good old USA, the maximum penalty for attempting to tamper with politicians in a "lobbying mechanism" would be life in prison without the possibility of parole.

We Must Gain Control in Congress

Once Occupiers gain a vast, veto-proof majority in Congress, the issue of campaign reform shall come with swiftness and clear focus. All campaign donations will be outlawed, becoming the equivalent of a felony if the contribution is at least one cent.

While all this might sound outlandish at face value, our clean, vibrant new system will rob the Wealthy of all their greedy power which now controls government.

Of course, there would be legitimate worries that Wealthy political candidates could finance their own political advertisements—giving themselves a huge campaign advantage over any 99-Percenter who might dare run against them. Any worries can easily get swept by the wayside, when we outlaw paid political advertising—which by its very nature has been corrupt and clearly designed to avoid directly focusing on issues.

If the government can outlaw cigarette advertising—which it has, it damn well can outlaw political advertising. You see, just like cigarettes, politics as we have known the system has been a cancerous affliction upon us all.

In an effort to circumvent these vital reforms, in an effort to retain their unfair political advantages, the Wealthy would seek to have the USA's corrupt courts system overturn all of the Occupy Movement's most vital reforms.

Remember that for the most part the U.S. judicial system including the nation's Supreme Court is not based on the "rule of law." Instead, the rulings hinge on varying ideologies, political loyalties and connections, and each judge's personal value systems.

This is a primary reason why many people become outraged with an obvious liberal or a conservative is nominated to the U.S. Supreme Court. Most educated people with any degree of common sense realize that major court rulings involving social and political issues have very little to do with the "law," but rather personal preferences.

We Need a Balanced Budget Amendment

To get around these obstacles, Occupy Activists nationwide and our future members in Congress will work to enact several amendments to the United States Constitution. First and foremost, the initial step will entail a Balanced Budget Amendment—preventing the federal government from becoming so large that it burdens business and people with onerous taxes and bureaucratic restrictions.

For political campaigns, candidates would be encouraged to go door-to-door and to meet at public gatherings including major events such as pre-scheduled debates.

No longer will the greasy politicians, especially at the Senate and the congressional house level, be able to hide from the public—which conducting only malicious, divisive and misleading political attack campaigns.

All along, the Rich and the 99-Percenters will enjoy unrestricted freedom of speech in the general media and at public gatherings. People everywhere would receive incentives to compete with the Wealthy-controlled mainstream media.

Also, partly in an effort to prevent "shady backroom political deals" or excessive favoritism in issuing federal contracts, another amendment to the Constitution would mandate that all U.S. government records are open to the public—except data involving ongoing criminal investigations and matters of national security.

An oversight committee would regularly review all such documentation, in order to determine which types of documents truly fall within the protected "top secret class."

Protect the Rights of Everyday Workers

Ideally, the Occupy party should strive to encourage the prosperity of business, while also fostering the need to protect the rights of everyday workers.

As we tear down cumbersome bureaucracy and whittle down the size of our federal government to a manageable form, we need to enact legislation that:

Tax breaks: Motivates employers that give their workers on-the-job training or outside formalized higher education.

Competition: More competition and entrepreneurship will help level the overall playing field at least somewhat, lessening the now-unbreakable power of Super Corporations.

Tax the rich: Especially because low-tax breaks for the Wealthy have failed to invigorate the economy in the past, raise the rates to more reasonable, higher levels for people earning more than $250,000 yearly.

Governmental loans: The federal government will be required to stay out of private business, never giving loans at taxpayer expense to huge corporations. The Solyndra case marks just one example of government run amuck, potential instances where politicians may have doled out taxpayer funds to benefit those who assisted them at getting elected.

The required changes in order to level the playing field between the wealthy and the poor will be formidable and challenging, but it can be done as long as the vast majority of Americans can become convinced to see the benefit of such efforts.

Give Unions Fair Bargaining Rights

An essential element in leveling the playing field, wiping away the unfair advantage of Corporate America, will be to give unions fair bargaining rights.

All along, we also must strive to keep U.S. industry as competitive, since the unstoppable fact remains that the economy has gone global. As Presidents Herbert Hoover and Calvin Coolidge learned all too late, any attempts to push back competitors—a process called "protectionism"—can and likely will cause extreme financial hardship for the entire American culture.

Rather than giving Big Companies tax breaks for shipping jobs overseas, as has been the case in recent decades, many huge firms will benefit from lower taxes throughout the United States.

In fact, under an additional focus, which will need much more study before possibly being enacted, companies will receive increasingly greater tax incentives the longer they keep top-rated, efficient and valuable employees rather than laying them off.

Meantime, via legislation more can and should be done to force U.S. corporations to pay their fair share of government-mandated taxes—rather than benefiting from a maze of complex loopholes. Within six weeks after our movement began, various mainstream media outlets reported that although the Untied States has a 35-percent corporate tax rate streams of huge firms are paying only an average 18.5 percent.

Eliminate the Securities Trading Advantage

While our tax overhaul gets underway, we will enact legislation outlawing the use of the Wealthy to use lightning-fast supercomputers to automatically trade securities—the process that now blocks the so-called little guy out of equal footing in the equities markets.

Much more important, in a significant development that should sharply boost the economy an additional constitutional amendment will ensure that the U.S. dollar is actually backed by gold and other precious metals such as silver. This will instantly bring greater credibility and strength to our national currency—which in recent years has seriously weakened in international markets. Until now, for the most part the American dollar has essentially been "worthless—having little value to back it up."

Going a step further, our Occupy legislators will:

Futures markets: Limit or outlaw the practice of pricing goods such as gasoline sold to consumers, based on totals the Forex traders predict can or will be at a future time. Instead, the price of goods, products or commodities within the marketplace will hinge on the basic laws of supply and demand, rather than backroom gimmickry.

Regulators: Work to ensure that the officials appointed to regulate or oversee the U.S. securities industry lack shady "good-old-boy" ties to the business sector that they're assigned to watch.

Health: Sever all ties between the federal Food and Drug Administration and the medical industry. Under the current process, due to close ties with FDA officials, pharmaceutical companies and physicians play a significant role in enacting regulations imposed upon the very industry that they benefit from—resulting in high costs to consumers.

Eliminate the Obamacare Program

The federal medical reform legislation known has "Obamacare" has significant flaws detrimental to both consumers and to the medical industry.

So far, the only entities that are positioned to benefit are the greedy huge medical insurance companies that have sharply boosted rates in recent years. Worsening matters, this abusive law scheduled to come on line in phases, would force or require regular folks to buy their own health insurance—or face severe financial fines enforced by the IRS.

Such legislation is tantamount to socialism, which sucks far worse than capitalism. The Obama-backed health fraud system would take Americans back to the dark ages, essentially worsening overall medical care.

History has taught us that all governments are inept, especially the federal bureaucracy. Our society is destined to failure if we think this goofy, overly complex legislation will help the average person.

The last thing each of us needs is for our government telling us how to manage our own health in a certain, bureaucratic way. Ultimately, only the Wealthy will benefit from this system, reaping in more profit from skyrocketing medical rates.

Largely as a result, coupled with the need to limit the size of government, the Occupy movement's primary objectives must and should include obliterating Obamacare.

Treat Front-Line Workers with Greater Dignity

Ultimately, if front-line American workers want more pay, they need to support a system that enables business to thrive—so that industry can pay higher salaries and better benefits. Any political philosophy or ideology that strives to essentially give workers a "free ride" for doing little or nothing is destined for severe failure.

At the same time, the United States also must simplify its burdensome tax code. By some accounts, a whopping 48 percent of Americans use loopholes to eventually pay no annual federal income taxes whatsoever. So, when complaining about the Rich, we also need to direct criticism at ourselves in this regard.

Some ultra-liberals whine that the Rich should pay higher taxes, when in fact a vast majority of the lower-income people end up paying nothing at all in federal taxes.

To level the playing field, the USA desperately needs an equitable and fair flat-tax system, one that's guaranteed never to creep up to higher levels thanks to the ultimately successful Balanced Budget Amendment.

Every step of the way, keep in mind that many of the nation's most respected economists will scoff at this overall plan. Why?

The simple answer rings true. Whether they'll admit this or not, the vast majority of today's most acclaimed economists—some of them working at Ivy League schools like Yale and Harvard—essentially work as sounding boards for Wealthy corporate America. Lots of these finance experts earn big bucks due to their seedy ties with industry, particularly grease-balls within the financial markets.

As a result, our most vibrant Occupy supporters will seek to engage with and to seek public comments from lesser-known but just as experienced or seasoned economists—those less likely to have seedy ties to 1-Percenters or to high-funded special interests.

CHAPTER 45
Power Shall Embolden Us to Positive Action

The many wrongs inflicted upon the poor by the wealthiest among us became so extensive and complex that to chronicle a basic list of wrongdoings would fill countless volumes. Suffice it to say that the sudden surge of Occupiers has put us on an unstoppable and unavoidable track to take positive action.

Although numerous fruitcakes and potheads among us likely will distort issues by generating violence or distorting the facts along the way, we shall eventually gain political power by:

Protests: Continually protesting, peacefully congregating while never letting our efforts fade away. This way, we'll continually remain in the public mindset.

Money: Occupy warriors will collect funds from our growing numbers of supporters to the point that we amass literally billions of dollars.

Message: We will continually communicate to the world that we realize our own weaknesses, but that far worse than us the Democratic and Republican parties of America are littered with corruption—too far on the liberal and conservative sides to do any solid "good" for our country.

Our Quest Might Take Decades to Achieve

The process of implementing effective change is likely to take many years, possibly decades. Every marathon runner starts his or her race with a mere single step.

Pushed into a sudden, widespread movement, as an overall group we've essentially hit the ground running—solidified in part thanks to social networking systems.

Taking every possible move to avoid violence and to denounce protestors who engage in pointless, unsanctioned violence, we can, should and must form our own political organization. Possibly named the Occupy Party, our group should advocate common-sense solutions rather than radical, off-the-wall strategies such as pushing for socialism or communism.

Such lunacy would never fly with the general populace, thereby making our overall efforts pointless. Therefore, within several years—if it hasn't been done so already—we need to elect leadership and develop a mission statement.

Meantime, just like any organization, a majority of those among us will disagree on many of our initial stands. Whatever the case, we must always remain aware of the vital, pressing need to form a political system that enables the average person to earn a decent living without having to work three or four jobs just to make ends meet.

Expect Troubling Times Along the Way

Invariably, as with almost every revolution of any important, along the way to reaching our objectives tragedies are likely to occur.

Without our consent, perhaps the lunatics among us will incite widespread, bloody riots and unnecessary carnage. Or, God forbid, a limited numbers of loony 1-Percenters might go so far as to have us physically and verbally attacked as an overall group.

The predictions of widespread carnage and destruction are quite plausible, when considering ever-increasing international food shortages and the weakening dollar. Adding to the crisis, recent surveys indicated that at least one out of 17 Americans is actually living at or below the poverty line, homeless and without enough to eat.

As the Wealthy sip champagne and dine on caviar, we show the world that the vast majority of 99-Percenters want to "earn our keep." We yearn to become educated and to perform at our chosen professions to the best of our abilities.

The inner-desires dictated by human nature tell us to live good, productive lives while caring as best we can for our children. We realize that the morals of society are crumbling virtually all around us, perhaps even more so than in any previous generation.

CHAPTER 46
Intensify the Revolution

To push our essential political process into full gear, all Occupy participants eagerly participate in regular ongoing annual events:

National Run-on-the-Banks Day: Actually held over a three-day period, this increasingly popular national event begins the second Wednesday of each May. From Wednesday through the following Friday, 99-Percenters across the United States and worldwide eagerly close their accounts at the major banks. The participants then eagerly open personal accounts at credit unions, financial institutions owned and operated by groups of people or organizations within local communities. Rather than answering to greedy corporate boards such as those running big greedy banks, credit unions are operated by regular folks. To find a credit union in your area, visit http://www.FindACreditUnion.com

National Dump-Stocks Day: Held the second Wednesday of every June, Occupy Warriors, their families and friends dump or unload their stock portfolios. This will result in a stock market crash, forcing Wealthy people to lose billions or perhaps trillions of dollars. Critics will complain that this process will shatter the world economy, but they should realize that the work environment around the globe has been shattered anyway. Some investors will view this day as a buying opportunity, yet that will not be the case

133

because under our process those who advocate our revolution will be permanently jumping from the markets—causing a permanent downturn in securities.

National Occupy Washington Day: Held the second Wednesday of each July, this glorious event will rival the famous 1969 Woodstock music festival in scope and magnitude. As this vital event builds in scope and importance from year to year, The Occupy Washington Day shall eventually draw many hundreds of thousands or perhaps even millions of people to our nation's capital. This will be a celebration of our size and power. When politicians whine about the cost of policing and cleaning up after the event, let the federal government pay because it has already screwed us big-time anyway.

National Join-a-Union Month: For the entire month of August, our membership will lobby hard in support of unions while encouraging people everywhere to join or participate in labor organizations—even those who are unemployed.

National Shun-the-Political-Parties Month: Throughout each September, our membership shall occupy local, state and national offices of the primary political parties that suck big time—the Democrats and the Republicans. All Occupy advocates should remember to keep these protests or gatherings peaceful, even if those organizations strive to make long-winded speeches in attempts to feed the general public a line of bull.

National Donate-to-the-Occupy-Movement Month: Throughout each October, we shall organize wide-scale, intense efforts to encourage people from all social classes and from a broad spectrum of professions to donate to certifiable and recognized organizations involving our cause. Ideally, members will organize, publicize and host legitimate, noteworthy grassroots fund-raising events such as arts shows and music festivals.

National Vote-the-Crooks-Out-of-Office Month: Each November, primarily during election years—of course—we strive individually and collectively to vote the worst crooks and most corrupt politicians out of office. To do this, everyone will have to do his or her own due diligence, since at this early stage virtually all long-term, long-standing politicians are corrupt—particularly those who have accepted significant campaign contributions.

National Feed-the-Hungry Month: During the height of the each December's holiday season, we work with local food banks and social service organizations to feed and shelter the many people left homeless or struggling by the greedy political and corporate policies of our nation's 1-Percenters.

National Peace Month: Throughout each January, we tell our "enemies," politicians and the 1-Percenters how much we truly and deeply love them despite their many failings—which we openly forgive. Rather than embracing hate and violence, we shall win the hearts and minds of at least some of them by taking the "high road."

National Occupy Recruiting Month: Every February, always with notable points such as Valentine's Day and President's Day, we work diligently to recruit new members. Realizing there is "strength in numbers," we strive year-round to encourage people to join our increasingly strong and well-organized movement.

National Spring Break Month: Everyone needs a rest. As college students party hard during their getaways from school, we'll use this period to re-energize and to solidify our short-term and long-term plans.

National Tax Deadline Month: When submitting our final income tax returns, usually due yearly on or around April 15, when a balance is due we always remit exactly one cent more than required. This will emerge as a logistical and paper nightmare for our inept national government. Rather than behaving like babies or immature punks, this is our sensible way of showing to the world that our national government is only worth one red cent at the very most.

While some of these monthly events or actions might seem insignificant, when considered collectively all these various tactics help play at least some role in making us strong—a force to be reckoned with. Even more effective, we can and should consider starting our own national credit union—preferably named the Occupy Credit Union. Eventually, a vast majority of people who support our cause could conduct all their financial transactions at Occupy Credit Unions, all focused on "helping the little guy."

Taking such a positive mode even further, we could launch Occupy Food Services, stores and entrepreneurial ventures—all of them designed to make money, but only for those willing to work hard enough to earn.

The workers in certified, recognized and fully affiliate Occupy Programs or companies could potentially generate high personal incomes and good retirements—depending on the financial performance of each venture.

Ideally, each venture would be owned by its own Occupy Workers, or the people who helped finance the start-ups—until such time as those individuals are paid back in full at low interest rates. Each venture would be run by and for its members, while striving to gain and retain competitiveness in the open marketplace.

Just as promising, some Occupy Firms could operate Research and Development—or R&D—divisions, designed to create, develop and implement new and profitable technology and business systems.

By gaining success in such ventures, Occupy participants will show themselves and the rest of the world that many of us appreciate capitalism when done correctly—without shuffling aside the basic needs and desires of average people.

CHAPTER 47
Keep Pressing Forward

Amid the coming struggles of our long local, national and international political battle, always strive to remain persistent and positive. Never give up.

An age-old saying tells us that "persistence is the twin sister of excellence. One is a matter of quality; the other, a matter of time."

Adhering to such truisms, let us work together throughout the coming generation and beyond to codify and learn from our mistakes and those of others. Through trial and error, we become stronger, better focused and even more strong-willed.

All along, we also should take great care to avoid becoming pig-headed. To gain effectiveness, any peaceful revolution requires at least some degree of compromise.

"A little more persistence, a little more effort, and what seems hopeless failure may turn to glorious success," said Elbert Hubbard, an American editor, publisher and writer in the late 19th and early 20th Centuries.

Seizing upon such boundless opportunities, we can and will gracefully and with great poise turn around the significant tide that has thus far crushed the middle class.

ABOUT THE AUTHORS

This book was written by vibrant and concerned participants in the Occupy Wall Street political and social movement.

www.ingramcontent.com/pod-product-compliance
Lightning Source LLC
Chambersburg PA
CBHW060907280326
41934CB00007B/1217